TABLE TALK

There's a celebrated story told of how Beatrice Lillie was dining once at Buckingham Palace when an unfortunate waiter spilled soup over her magnificent gown. For a moment a dreadful silence descended as everyone glared at the wretched man, then Miss Lillie rescued the situation by turning to him and saying with mock severity, 'Never darken my Dior again.'

The French novelist and playright Tristan Bernard had a particular antipathy towards women journalists. He certainly didn't warm to the one he was next to at a press lunch who said as they took their seats. 'Forget I am a woman. Treat me as you would a male colleague.'

Throughout the meal Bernard totally ignored her. Only when lunch was finished did he turn to her and say, *'Allons pisser'*

Derek Nimmo's

Table Talk
A Witty Companion
for Winers and Diners

CORONET BOOKS
Hodder and Stoughton

Copyright © 1990
Derek Nimmo

First published in Great Britain in
1990 by Robson Books Ltd.

Coronet edition 1991

British Library C.I.P.

Nimmo Derek
  Table talk.
  I. Title
  641.01

  ISBN 0-340-55764-8

Printed and bound in Great
Britain for Hodder and Stough-
ton Paperbacks, a division of
Hodder and Stoughton Limited,
Mill Road, Dunton Green,
Sevenoaks, Kent TN13 2YA
(Editorial Office: 47 Bedford
Square, London WC1B 3DP) by
Clays Ltd., St Ives plc.

Contents

Introduction

There's an apochryphal story that I've always rather enjoyed in which a young second lieutenant goes to join his regiment and is greeted by the colonel with words of welcome. 'We're so pleased to have you with us,' says the colonel. 'I do hope you enjoy the mess. On Monday night we have mess night with all the chaps. There's a lot of drinking and you'll find it frightfully good fun.'

'I'm sorry, sir. I don't drink,' the lieutenant told him.

'Oh, really? Well ...Wednesday night. You'll like that. We always have a dance. There are lots of very pretty girls. You'll really enjoy that.'

'No, sir,' said the lieutenant. 'I don't go in for that sort of thing.'

'Really? Are you homosexual?' asked the colonel.

'No, sir!'

'In that case you won't enjoy Friday night either.'

As it so happens, my own interest and devotion to the pleasures of the table in their many forms were first kindled against a military background – though, I hasten to add, in rather less rarified surroundings. Recently I discovered that the event is totally documented. The entry in my diary for 19 September 1951 reads, 'Celebrated my birthday. Drank a bottle of Commanderia. Became inebriated.' At eighteen I was even more pompous than I am now.

I had just arrived in Cyprus as a young national serviceman and was quite overwhelmed, coming from a very austere, rationed Great Britain, to find myself in a land overflowing with wine and honey. Not that Commanderia was necessarily the ideal introductory tipple for a tentative toper. This dessert wine was apparently originally constructed (and I use the word advisedly) during the Crusades by the Knights Hospitaller of the Order of St John of Jerusalem from the vines of Kilossi Castle in Cyprus. I have always thought that perhaps the Knights were a trifle over-hospitable and that this largely contributed to the retake of the Holy Land.

Be that as it may, since that fateful day in Famagusta nearly forty years ago, I have spent a great deal of my time researching, discovering and above all enjoying wine (while fostering more than a passing acquaintance with the many-splendoured dishes that complement it around the world).

St Paul visited Cyprus and may also have become similarly enthused. It was perhaps after a night on the Commanderia that he wrote his instruction to Timothy: 'Drink no longer water but use a little wine for thy stomach's sake.' It has certainly always seemed to me to be a frightfully good idea and an injunction which I have earnestly tried to heed over the years. Particularly if my stomach is going to be helped by a bottle of Château Petrus.

Such has been my enthusiasm for the subject that I am in danger of becoming a major bore on the matter. My wife would say that I already am. I have written a couple of books on my favourite tipples – both of which you can find remaindered at any bad bookshop. I am a member of the Wine Guild of Great Britain, the Jourade of St Emilion and Chief Mate of Millawa, an Australian Wine Order of dubious distinction.

We live in an exciting time for lovers of good food and wine. Having long carried a torch for the many excellent wines produced in Australia, I discovered something every bit as promising last year in Seoul. This was a superb sparkling wine produced by the *méthode champenoise* under the supervision of Deutz, the French champagne house. The grapes of the vines had been planted on the same latitude as and on similar soil to Epernay. Korean wine could perhaps be the next big discovery. One wonders what Korean cuisine might have on the menu. My recollection is of a predilection for cabbage – but that's another story.

Here I have gathered together a collection of anecdotes and stories that have appealed to me, along with some interesting insights into the culinary careers of some of the great winers and diners of the past – plus a few Nimmo favourites that I couldn't resist slipping in.

To return to biblical authority, if I may (the Book of Ecclesiastes this time), we read: 'Then I commended mirth, because a man hath no better thing under the sun, than to eat, and to drink and to be merry: for that shall abide with him of his labour the days of his life.'

I can do no better than say 'Amen' to that.

Will you join me?

Food for Thought

Allow me to let you into a little secret.

Once upon a time, a long while ago, I used to turn an honest penny serving hamburgers and the occasional hot dog at an establishment run by the estimable Mr Forte in the West End of London. This temporary change of career direction was prompted by the need for the aforementioned honest penny, of which there was a noticeable dearth during one period of being rather heavily out of work on the stage.

This particular snack bar may have been of fairly humble character but I like to think that I played my part in the manner of the maître d'hôtel of the Savoy. Not that I was alone in my endeavours. Anton Rogers, finding himself similarly relieved of professional engagements, was my willing cohort and together we offered a service of which, I think, Mr Forte would have been justly proud.

He may have been less happy about the returns. In a spirit of unstinting philanthropy, we did every so often find ourselves handing out the odd free sausage and bun to resting actor chums, whose need for the occasional free bite was every bit as great as our own.

In return for £6 a week (plus tips) I devoted

myself wholeheartedly to the creation of the finest hamburgers and hot dogs west of Soho. It seemed, too, that I achieved some modest success in this self-appointed task. One day I was taken tremulously aside by one of Mr Forte's area managers, who kindly expressed to me the thought that I might be capable of some more important function in life than slapping a bit of hot mince in the middle of a warm bun.

He offered to groom me for stardom! It seemed that the paternalistic Mr Forte was on the lookout for likely lads to be trained in the complexities of catering in general and *haute cuisine* in particular. Would I care to become one of a select number destined for a course in hotel management in Italy?

It was one of those rare moments in life when, at the drop of a chef's hat one could easily have wandered off into avenues new. In exchange for selling one's sole for a dollop of Scampi Frite, I could by now perhaps be chief pastry cook at the Café Royal, or head chef at the Heston Services on the M4.

Foolishly I declined his charming offer, pledging my life to the ceaseless improvement of the noble hamburger. That selfless act of devotion won me modest promotion to selling the same in Battersea Pleasure Gardens.

Life has moved on since then. So, I imagine, has the hamburger. But food and its preparation have always held an important place in my affections.

I am fortunate enough to count Anton Edelmann among my friends and one of my great joys is to be invited to dine at the chef's table at the Savoy, where one can watch the whole kitchen brigade at

14

full stretch as the orders begin to come in for lunch. The proceedings are conducted entirely in French, even though most of the staff are English. To watch 120 people working in unison like this, as a time and motion exercise, is one of the most exciting things you can see.

Taking plays to hotels all over the world, I have developed a great affinity with kitchen staff from Adelaide to Abuja (about which more later). One of the first of these theatrical offerings was *Why Not Stay for Breakfast?*, which we opened in Hong Kong. Since we were performing in the main dining-room, the actors had to parade through the kitchens to the stage (as is usually the case with these hotel shows). In this instance the girl in the play with me had to be eight months pregnant in the first act, in order to have the baby in the second. All the Chinese chefs were very solicitous in assisting her through their domain to the stage. So it came as some surprise to them when she made her way through the kitchen only a short time later having had it. They were even more amazed on the second night when she reappeared every bit as pregnant, to pass inscrutably through their midst once again.

The English breakfast has long been a source of envy and, in some cases, bewilderment to visitors to these shores. Lady Colin Campbell, writing in her *Etiquette of Good Society* in 1893, was moved to comment, 'I must say that our breakfast tables are more inviting and present a more elegant appearance than did those of our ancestors. Delicate and refined habits of eating have replaced the coarse eating of the Middle Ages.'

One shudders to think what she might have made of what passes for breakfast in many households today compared with her own generous offerings:

Spring

Broiled trout
Codfish cakes
Curried eggs
Savoury Omelette
Potted char
Potted beef
Stewed kidneys
Pommes de terre frites

Ox-palates
Marmalade
Water cresses

Pigeon pie
Ham
Spiced beef

Autumn

Broiled fresh herrings
Collared eels
Poached eggs
Potted hare
Potted lobster
Toasted mushrooms
Broiled pheasant
Reindeer-tongue

Fresh shrimps
Grapes

Grouse pie
Cold roast fowl
Ham
Rolled beef

King Edward VII used to start the day with a modest five-course breakfast. Eggs came first — poached, scrambled, or served as an omelette. Bacon followed. His Majesty liked his bacon cut into large, thick slices, so large in fact that there wasn't room for eggs and bacon on the same plate. These preliminaries out of the way, he moved into a fish course — turbot, lobster or salmon, as the mood took him. This would be followed by a steak or a couple of chops. And to round off the meal he enjoyed a little game or poultry.

So the royal gastronomic day began. It provided a fitting prelude to the ten-course lunch which awaited His Majesty every day at one o'clock sharp.

In *The Gourmet's Guide to Europe* the authors, Lieutenant-Colonel Newnham-Davis and Algernon Bastard, offered the following suggestion for breakfasting in Venice at the beginning of this century:

Begin with a Vermouth Amaro in lieu of a cocktail. For hors d'oeuvre have some small crabs cold, mashed up with sauce tartare and a slice or two of *prosciutto crudo* (raw ham), cut as thin as cigarette paper. After this some cutlets done in the Bologna style, a thin slice of ham on top, and hot parmesan and grated white truffles and *fegato alla veneziana* complete the repast except for a slice of *stracchino* cheese. A bottle of

Val Policella is exactly suited to this kind of repast and a glass of fine Champagne and of ruby-coloured Alkermes for the lady, if your wife accompanies you, make a good ending.

The Maître d'Hôtel will be interested in you directly he finds that you know how a man should breakfast.

Anyone tempted to duck out of breakfast should avoid the hotel in the German port of Bremen which at one time carried in every room the admonition, 'Breakfast ist obligatory.'

When rationing was introduced during the Great War few households can have exercised it more diligently than that of the Royal Family. Late arrivers at breakfast frequently found the dishes cleared of food by those who had risen before them. One morning a member of the King's staff who had been detained by a telephone call arrived at the table and found nothing to eat. Summoning a footman, he asked if he could be brought a boiled egg.

To the ears of George V this was tantamount to treason. Setting down his cutlery, he turned on the wretched courtier, accusing him of betraying his country and of being a slave to his stomach. He hinted darkly that the war might be lost and the empire crumble as a direct result of his greed.

Dean Swift spent a Thursday night in an Irish monastery and at breakfast the next morning tucked into eggs and bacon while his monastic hosts ate fish.

Determined not to let him get away with this, the monks offered up the grace: 'From bacon and eggs and rotten legs [Swift was a little shaky on his pins], good Lord deliver us.'

Swift was quick to respond: 'From oysters and cockles and men without bottles, good Lord deliver us.' Then, going one better, he continued:

> Does any man of common sense
> Think ham and eggs give God offence?
> Or that a herring has a charm
> The Almighty's anger to disarm?
> Wrapped in His majesty divine,
> D'you think He cares on what we dine?

In between her detailed instructions to the mistress of the well-managed Victorian home and recipes for breathtaking numbers of guests calmly itemized and described (sometimes, one suspects, to her reader's mounting horror and dismay), Mrs Beeton did allow herself moments of light relief, of which this exchange is one:

Lord Bacon was about to pass sentence of death on a man of the name of Hogg, when the prisoner said with an expression of arch confidence, 'I claim indulgence, my lord, on the plea of relationship; for I am convinced your lordship will never be unnatural enough to hang one of your own family.'

'Indeed,' replied the judge with some amazement. 'I was not aware that I had the honour of your alliance. Perhaps you will be good enough to name the degree of your affinity.'

'My name, my lord, is Hogg,' replied the impudent thief. 'Your lordship's is Bacon, and all then will allow that bacon and hog are very closely allied.'

'I am sorry,' replied his lordship. 'I cannot allow the truth of your insistence. Hog cannot be bacon until it is hanged. So before I can admit your plea, or acknowledge the family compact, Hogg must be hanged tomorrow morning.'

The language of food can lead to much innocent fun. Take this engaging American recipe for peanut-butter-grilled corn:

Husk fresh corn; spread ears lightly with peanut butter. Wrap each ear with bacon slice; fasten with toothpick. Place on grill, turning until done – about ten minutes. Or let everyone grill his own ears, using long skewers to do so.

Faced with an onslaught of American fast food, burgeoning oriental cuisine and mixed messages from Continental kitchens (not to mention BSE), many an Englishman may be forgiven for harking back to the days when there was only one food to tempt his palate. Here it is, celebrated in song.

The Roast Beef of Old England
When mighty roast beef was the Englishman's food,
It ennobled our hearts, and enriched our blood;
Our soldiers were brave, and our courtiers were good.
Oh, the roast beef of old England!
And oh, for old England's roast beef!

But since we have learnt from effeminate France
To eat their ragouts as well as to dance,
We are fed up with nothing but vain complaisance.
Oh, the roast beef, etc.

Our fathers of old were robust, stout and strong,
And kept open house with good cheer all day long,
Which made their plump tenants rejoice in the song.
Oh, the roast beef, etc.

When good Queen Elizabeth sat on the throne,
Ere coffee, tea, and such slip-slops were known,
The world was in terror if e'er she did frown.
Oh, the roast beef, etc.

In those days if fleets did presume on the main,
They seldom, or never return'd back again,

As witness the vaunting Armada of Spain.
Oh, the roast beef, etc.

Oh, when we had stomachs to eat and to fight,
And when wrongs were cooking, to set ourselves
right;
But now we're a-hm! – I could, but good night.
Oh, the roast beef, etc.

Having recently returned from Latin America, I can confirm that imports of Scotch whisky still far outstretch those for other Scottish foodstuffs. This might account in part for the confusion of customs officials in the Brazilian city of São Paolo, who, several years ago, were slightly nonplussed when confronted by a haggis that arrived on a flight from these shores. They wisely resorted to chemical analysis before deciding to admit it duty-free under the classification 'Unscheduled horticultural fertilizer'.

Fair fa' your honest sonsie face,
Great chieftain o' the puddin'–race!
Aboon them a' ye tak your place,
Painch, tripe, or thairm:
Weel are ye worthy o' a grace
As lang's my arm.

Burns may have written to the haggis – but then, I don't suppose he's that widely read in São Paolo either.

Men have disposed of their wives for a variety of reasons down the years. Few, I venture to suggest, have murdered two wives because of their short-comings in the kitchen. Such was the fate, however, of the unfortunate Mesdames Carriou, wives of one M Noël Carriou, whose culinary expectations were exacting even by French standards.

Mme Carriou (*numéro un*) fell foul of her husband because she persistently served his roast too rare. Driven beyond the point of self-control, he threw her so violently out of bed after yet another red-blooded joint that the poor lady broke her neck. That act of impetuosity earned him a prison sentence, reduced to seven years with good conduct. He tried marrying a second time.

Twelve years later Mme Carriou (*numéro deux*) met a similar fate when she veered to the other extreme in the roasting pan and presented her husband with one overcooked joint too many.

In due course M Noël Carriou was arraigned once more. Cleared of murder by a sympathetic jury, he was given eight years for manslaughter.

Passing sentence, the judge acknowledged that the quality of the cooking is an important part of marriage.

The Revd Sydney Smith, Dean of St Paul's and conceiver of many a *bon mot*, indulged a late-eighteenth-century parson's passion for food and wine (and I put it no stronger than that). 'My idea of heaven,' he used to say, 'is eating *pâté de fois gras* to the sound of trumpets.' His attention to detail with humbler fare was no less punctilious. Creating a salad, for instance, moved him to verse:

> To make this condiment, your poet begs
> The pounded yellow of two hard-boiled eggs,
> Two boiled potatoes, passed through kitchen-sieve,
> Smoothness and softness to the salad give;
> Let onion atoms lurk within the bowl,
> And, scarce-suspected, animate the whole.
> Of mordant mustard add a single spoon,
> Distrust the condiment that bites so soon;
> But deem it not, thou man of herbs, a fault,
> To add a double quantity of salt.
> Add, lastly, o'er the flavoured compound toss
> A magic soup-spoon of anchovy sauce.
> On, green and glorious! Oh, herbaceous treat!
> 'Twould tempt the dying anchorite to eat;

Back to the world he'd turn his fleeting soul.
And plunge his fingers in the salad bowl!
Serenely full, the epicure would say,
Fate cannot harm me, I have dined today.

The great landscape artist Joseph Mallord William Turner was equally discerning when it came to salads. Presented with one at table, he observed to his neighbour, 'Nice cool green, that lettuce, isn't it? And the beetroot pretty red – not quite strong enough; and the mixture, delicate tint of yellow that. Add some mustard, and then you have one of my pictures.'

At one stage in his life Beau Brummell went through a phase of eschewing all vegetables. Asked by a lady whether he had ever eaten any, the leader of the Regency beau monde replied, 'Yes, madam. I once ate a pea.'

A correspondent to the *Sunday Dispatch* sixty odd years ago expressed misgivings about public hygiene and wrote, 'When I pointed out the folly of a male shop assistant who was coughing and sneezing near an exposed keg of butter without using a handkerchief, the young lady serving me replied, "Oh, it isn't butter, it's margarine."'

Confusion over cooking instructions can lead to unfortunate mishaps in any kitchen. A few years ago one such misunderstanding occurred between the official body in charge of tagging migratory birds in the United States of America and a farmer in the state of Arkansas. The farmer, out with his gun one day, shot one of the tagged birds as it passed over his land and took it home for the pot. Finding a tag on its leg, his wife mistook these for cooking instructions – which she followed. But when supper was served, the bird was less than satisfying. Closer inspection revealed that the words on the tag were the abbreviation for the Washington-based wildlife research survey: *Wash. Biol. Surv.*

Recent food-poisoning scares that have swirled around the incorrect handling of cook-chill foods and frozen poultry might lead one to the mistaken belief that they are something new. Nothing could be further from the truth. In 1626 a chilled chicken indirectly carried off the philosopher and statesman Francis Bacon.

Out for a drive in his carriage one snowy March day with Dr Witherbone, physician to King Charles I, a breakthrough in food science suddenly dawned on the ever-inventive Bacon. As John Aubrey recorded in *Brief Lives*, ' . . . it came into my Lord's thoughts, why flesh might not be preserved in snow as in salt'.

Without further ado he stopped the carriage in the fields near the bottom of Highgate Hill, went to a nearby cottage and bought a hen. Having killed and drawn this, he and Dr Witherbone stuffed the carcass with snow.

Aubrey fails to mention how the chicken fared, for his attention turned to poor Bacon. He caught such a shocking chill in the process and became so ill that he could not go home, retiring instead to the Earl of Arundel's house at Highgate. Bed was what he needed and bed he was given – though it turned out that the bed had not been aired for a good year and indeed was so damp that Bacon's condition deteriorated drastically and he died of pneumonia inside three days.

In the days before salmonella became a household word the author of *A New System of Domestic Cookery* offered this advice on choosing eggs at market:

> Put the large end of the egg to your tongue; if it feels warm it is new. In new-laid eggs, there is a small division of the skin from the shell, which is filled with air, and is perceptible to the eye at the end. On looking through them against the sun or a candle, if fresh, eggs will be pretty clear. If they shake they are not fresh.

If Napoleon Bonaparte was right about an army marching on its stomach, one wonders what he would have had to say about the bill of fare advertised at a Hampshire bus station, which offered its patrons (among other things): Egg and Chips; Two Eggs and Chips; Egg, Bacon and Chips; Two Eggs, Bacon and Chips; Sausage and Chips; Two Sausages and Chips; Bacon, Sausage and Chips; Eggs, Sausage and Chips; Egg, Two Sausages and Chips; Two Eggs, Sausage and Chips; Two Eggs, Two Sausages and Chips; Two Eggs, Bacon, Two Sausages and Chips; Egg, Bacon, Sausage, Beefburger and Chips...

From 1835 until 1848 Austria was ruled by Emperor Ferdinand I, a sovereign whose weakness of mind and regular bouts of insanity reduced the empire to a state of anarchy that led to his abdication in favour of his nephew Francis Joseph. Little is recorded of Ferdinand's years on the throne, but what is probably his most enduring remark has entered the annals: 'I am the emperor,' he once averred, 'and I want dumplings.'

The somewhat sceptical light in which our Continental neighbours tend to view British cuisine can only have been reinforced by our national offering at the thirteenth Foire Gastonomique held at Dijon, thankfully some years ago now. A correspondent to *The Times* wrote afterwards that, 'The British stand (a poor thing, but our own) was displaying, among other national delicacies, tins of cat and dog food.'

The banquets thrown by oriental potentates catered for some bizarre tastes and, reading certain recipes, one could be forgiven for wondering whether they might not sit a trifle uncomfortably in a European stomach. A dish favoured by several

Indian princes required the cooks to take a whole camel, put a goat inside this, and inside the goat to put a peacock. The peacock was then stuffed with a chicken, which in turn was filled with a sand-grouse, inside which was a quail stuffed with a sparrow. When the dish was ready, the camel was put in a hole in the ground and steamed!

The mysteries of Chinese food were rather engagingly captured in the verses written by a long-established English resident in Canton, who wrote of a fellow countryman's very tentative tasting of the strange delicacies laid before him. Eventually he found something he recognized:

> And he thought himself in luck
> When close before him what he saw
> Looked something like a duck!
> Still cautious grown, but to be sure,
> His brain he set to rack.
> At length he turned to one behind,
> And pointing cried, 'Quack, quack?'
> The Chinese gravely shook his head,
> Next made a reverend bow,
> And then expressed what dish it was
> By uttering, 'Bow-wow-wow!'

Among the great Victorian gastronomes few showed a spirit of adventure and curiosity greater than that of the Bucklands, *père et fils*. William Buckland was an eminent geologist and Reader of Mineralogy at the University of Oxford. He also exhibited an extraordinary taste for unconventional foods. Crocodile, hedgehog and mole all passed his lips, the latter being awarded the accolade of the most disgusting thing he had ever tasted. That was until he sampled bluebottles.

Perhaps William Buckland's most singular gastronomic coup came about when his friend Edward Harcourt, Archbishop of York, showed him the embalmed heart of Louis XIV. He had bought this in Paris during the French Revolution and kept it in a snuff box. Buckland looked at it with interest, commented, 'I have eaten some strange things, but never the heart of a king', and then picked it out of the box and swallowed it!

His culinary crusade was taken up by his son Frank. He was a founder member of the worthy Society for the Acclimatization of Animals in the United Kingdom, a body established to counter food shortages by broadening the range of the British diet. At one of the Society's dinners, guests were treated to bird's nest soup, Japanese sea-slug, kangaroo, wild boar and curassow from Central America.

His enthusiasms were by no means universal. After eating his way through a horseflesh dinner that included horse tongue, soup and sausages, not to mention horse joints, a roast baron of horse and boiled withers, Frank Buckland's verdict was, 'Hippophagy has not the slightest chance of suc-

31

cess in this country.'

Neither he nor his father was a crank, however. Frank's concern with food production led to his appointment as inspector of salmon fisheries, and in 1870 he was made special commissioner of salmon fisheries in Scotland.

A memo circulated in the Middlesex Hospital catering department and subsequently highlighted by *World Medicine* advised: 'Patients wishing to order Pancakes should tick the box marked Apple Flan & Custard and likewise patients ordering Jelly and Ice Cream should mark the Fruit Salad box.'

A cookery book may not seem the most likely stimulus for one's final will and testament yet a lady from Philadelphia was thus inspired, for under the heading 'Chili Sauce without Working' in the cookery book of Mrs Maggie North of Philadelphia ran the following:

> 4 quarts of ripe tomatoes, 4 small onions, 4 green peppers, 2 teacups of sugar, 2 quarts of cider vinegar, 2 ounces ground allspice, 2 ounces cloves, 2 ounces cinnamon, 12 teaspoonfuls salt.

Chop tomatoes, onions and peppers fine, add the rest mixed together and bottle cold. Measure tomatoes when peeled. In case I die before my husband I leave everything to him.

It is pleasing to see that British bakers are making some inroads, however modest, into the traditional German bastions of *Kuchen* and *Torten*. An English visitor admiring the assorted cakes and gâteaux teaux on display in a cake shop in northern Germany was pleased to see one bearing the legend, 'English "Lady Cake" '. This was defined as 'Plum Cake mit Whisky'.

Mrs Rundell, the author of *A New System of Domestic Cookery* (1818), was a lady of considerable ingenuity and, if this tip is anything to go by, one who displayed an admirable sense of economy in the kitchen:

> *To Make Sprats Taste Like Anchovies*
> Salt them well and let the salt drain from them. In 24 hours wipe them dry, but do not wash them. Mix 4 oz of common salt, 1 oz of bay salt, 1 oz saltpetre, ½ oz of sal-prunel and half a

teaspoon of cochineal, all in the finest powder. Sprinkle it among 3 quarts of the fish, and pack them in two stone jars. Keep in a cool place, fastened down with a bladder. These are pleasant on bread and butter, but use the best for sauce.

Synthetic foods have always taken a while to be accepted and some, like the Sitwell egg, never progress beyond the prototype. In the case of the latter, this is rather a shame, for it was an example of the uniquely creative spirit of Sir George Sitwell, father of Edith, Osbert and Sacheverell.

The eponymous egg he conceived was destined to be a handy, portable snack for travellers – a sort of thinking-man's Scotch egg, if you like. There was to be a 'yolk' of smoked meat, a 'white' of compressed rice and a shell of synthetic lime. However, the Sitwell egg never got beyond the office of Mr Gordon Selfridge, the founder of the Oxford Street shop that bears his name. Sir George had decided that he should be entrusted with marketing his invention and he duly presented himself unannounced in Mr Selfridge's office one morning, complete with egg. The fact that the Sitwell egg was scarcely ever referred to again after that encounter suggests that Mr Selfridge's enthusiasm fell some way short of Sir George's.

At Your Service

One of the most courteous gestures one encounters when dining in Hong Kong is the practice of sprinkling stains from a teapot on your tablecloth before you sit down. It means you can make as much mess as you like without dissolving into a lather of perspiration every time you drop something and spares the nervous and surreptitious wiping and covering with napkins which might otherwise be called for.

To the uninitiated, sitting down to eat in unfamiliar surroundings can be a thoroughly unnerving experience. Not long ago I was present at a gathering in Nigeria where goat soup was served. Few parts of the carcass failed to make it into the pot and I was more than a little taken aback when I caught sight of a floating curried willy slowly coming towards me.

Not that exotic tastes are confined to foreign climes. Thirty years ago I was on tour with Vivien Leigh when we stayed in a slightly seedy hotel where grouse appeared on the menu one evening. As I recall, the place was run by a retired colonel who maintained, 'There's only one thing to have after grouse – sardines in gin!', which wasn't the sort of thing that I'd immediately have thought of.

So he poured out about half a bottle of gin for the occasional sardine to swim around in. This he then set alight, serving me with the only flambéd sardines I have ever eaten. At the time it seemed quite amusing, but after all these years it probably isn't all that unusual; food has changed such a lot in this country.

Knowing what to wear for dinner can be a little tricky, too. As one of a group of house guests at a friend's country seat, I well remember the potential embarrassment of a delightful Australian couple who came down to dinner wearing a lounge suit (and female equivalent) to find the rest of the company in black tie. Our host sized up the situation instantly, shot back up to his room and reappeared in the scruffiest tweeds he could find. Antipodean blushes were spared.

However, through no one's fault it did turn out to be a slightly unsettling evening for them all round. It so happens that John, my chauffeur-cum-butler, adores dressing up and our host, who has always had a soft spot for him, had invited him to look through the old family livery room to see whether there was anything he would like to wear to serve at dinner. John was very taken with a magnificent yellow footman's livery from the last century. They were a bit short of jabots but our host had been either Lord Lieutenant of the County or Sheriff, and had a jabot left over from his official kit which he was able to lend John. Alongside the other staff dressed in black, I must say that he did cut quite a dash. The Australian couple clearly thought so when greeted by this apparition as we went in to dinner.

Then, as luck would have it, the lights in that entire part of the county failed as dinner was drawing to a close and the house and surrounding countryside were plunged into Stygian darkness. Our hostess went in search of candles and, while the brightest of these were used to illuminate the bridge tables in the drawing-room, I sat and talked to the Australian guests. The circumstances seemed ideally suited to the telling of ghost stories and I launched into one of my favourites, fortified by an excellent dinner and fine wines. The hour was late and I was pleasantly amused by my listeners' visible unease as my tale unfolded. Indeed, I had just finished when John appeared out of the gloom, eerily resplendent in his footman's clothes and bearing a guttering candle to light my Australian friends along blackened corridors and up benighted stairs to bed.

When they came down to breakfast the next morning we noticed that they looked a little shamefaced and it emerged that they had been so thoroughly disturbed by my ghost story and their pitch-black bedroom, which I must confess did bear more than a passing resemblance to the one in my tale, that almost as soon as John had departed with his guttering candle, they had retreated to another room. How right Milton was when he observed, 'They also serve who only stand and wait.'

❋

In her autobiography of Alice B Toklas, Gertrude Stein tells the story of Miss Stein's cook-cum-housekeeper, a redoubtable lady by the name of Hélène.

Hélène, it appeared, had a very strict sense of what was right and proper, especially where her fellow countrymen were concerned. Foreigners she might forgive for an unthinking lapse in etiquette, but never a Frenchman. Matisse apparently committed one such cardinal error – and paid the price. Visiting Miss Stein one day, he inquired of Hélène what was for dinner. She told him and later found that he was staying unexpectedly to partake of it. In Hélène's eyes that was a bit thick and she marked Matisse down for censure when the occasion arose.

That time came when Miss Stein next announced that Matisse would be joining her for dinner. Hélène's response was masterful and damning. In that case, she avowed, she would not make an omelette as she had planned, but would fry the eggs instead. The ingredients would be the same, she informed Miss Stein, but fried eggs showed less respect than an omelette. Matisse, she knew, would understand the significance.

Cooking for the poet and essayist Walter Savage Landor was a nerve-racking occupation. Landor's irascible temper led to frequent quarrels and on one occasion a cook who presented him with a meal that failed to please him was seized and thrown through an open window. Landing awkwardly in the flowerbed below, the cook broke his arm. Hearing his calls for help, Landor looked out and exclaimed, 'Good God, I forgot the violets!'

Restaurant staff, tiring of abusive customers, took it upon themselves to strike back. Several years ago a notice appeared in a Channel Islands restaurant: 'If you like home cooking – stay home.'

More chilling was the warning spotted in a northern café: 'Complaints to the cook can be hazardous to your health.'

Sussex teashops may not immediately spring to mind at the mention of self-service catering. However, when a couple of visitors to one of these establishments ordered tea – one with milk, the other with lemon – the waitress taking their order pointed out that if they wanted lemon with their tea, they would have to nip into the shop next door and buy one.

Having squeezed into a restaurant well after last orders had been taken and having persuaded the staff to find him something to eat, Gilbert Harding was polishing off the last mouthful when his ear caught one of the waiters confiding to a colleague in amazement, 'He's eaten it!'

On the subject of table manners, Colette wrote in *Gigi*, 'The three great stumbling-blocks in a girl's education...are *homard à l'Américaine*, a boiled egg, and asparagus', adding, 'Shoddy table manners have broken up many a happy home.'

The author of *Manners and Rules of Good Society* shared her anxiety and offered this advice a century ago:

Soup should be eaten with a table spoon, and not with a dessert. (In these days no one 'drinks' soup: it is 'eaten'.) Fish should be eaten with a silver fish-knife and fork. All made dishes, such as *rissoles*, patties, etc should be eaten with a fork only. In eating asparagus a knife and fork should be used. Salad should be eaten with a knife and fork. Peas should be eaten with a fork. Jellies, blancmanges, iced puddings, etc. should be eaten with a fork, as should all sweets sufficiently substantial to admit of it.

When eating cheese, small morsels of the cheese should be placed with a knife on small morsels of bread, and the two conveyed to the mouth with the thumb and finger, the piece of bread being the morsel to hold as cheese should not be taken up in the fingers, and should be eaten off the point of the knife.

As a matter of course, young ladies should not eat cheese at dinner-parties.

Nowhere can precedence or protocol have been more scrupulously observed than in India during the heyday of the Raj. The Duke of Windsor once commented that he hadn't realized what royalty was until, as Prince of Wales, he stayed at Government House in Bombay in 1921.

Then there was the unhappy experience of a young wife, eager to please her husband and impress their hosts, who received a sharp rebuke for wearing gloves at dinner in the jungle.

The order of dishes was a carefully regulated affair in nineteenth-century dinners. Here is *The Servants' Guide and Family Manual* on the subject:

The order of taking up is the first dish by the Butler, and the remainder of the fish and soups by the Under Butler and Footman . . . The cook is apprized of the serving of the soups and fish by the Butler ringing the dining-room bell; the removes or first course are then got ready; the soup and fish are conveyed out of the room by the Footman, who likewise brings up the next course which is placed upon the table with the same precision as were the soups and fish; the several dishes being placed on, and removed from off the table, by the Butler, and taken from him by the Footman.

During the last century beer formed an important part of a servant's pay. Men servants could reckon on receiving three pints a day; the women two pints. This was provided more to keep the domestic staff strong than keep them sweet. Though not all servants welcomed this provision. Back in the 1880s a 'member of the aristocracy' expressed some concern when discussing beer in his or her handy little volume on the handling of servants. 'Women servants, on the contrary, invariably dispense with beer altogether,' the warning reads, 'whereas they would probably be stronger if they did not deprive themselves of it.'

So much for drink being the curse of the working classes.

A charming example of the consideration and courtesy displayed by the best employers to their staff was shown several years ago now by the case of a retired farrier living in Rochdale. He had once held the post of Royal Farrier and ruled the roost in the stables at Hampton Court. Though retired for several years, few Christmases passed without his receiving a plum pudding wrapped in velvet, sent with the good wishes of the Royal Family.

There's a celebrated story told of how Beatrice Lillie was dining once at Buckingham Palace when an unfortunate waiter spilled soup over her magnificent evening-gown. For a moment a dreadful silence descended as everyone glared at the wretched man, then Miss Lillie rescued the situation by turning to him and saying with mock severity, 'Never darken my Dior again.'

Kenneth Williams used to tell the story of the time when he was stranded in Gibraltar while travelling to Morocco. Having a drink in his hotel bar he got into conversation with a couple of chaps whom he took for fellow travellers similarly delayed. However, it turned out that they were members of the crew of the aircraft carrier *Eagle* – one a signalman, the other a leading stoker.

Kenneth was chatting away with this pair when a waiter whispered in his ear that he was wanted on the telephone. On the other end of the line was his friend the restaurateur Johnny Koon, who was opening a new Chinese restaurant in Gibraltar that night and wanted Kenneth to cut the ribbon and say a few words. He'd invited the *The Times of Gibraltar*, along with the governor and the commander-in-chief of the garrison. It sounded fun and Kenneth said he'd love to join them, adding that he'd just met a couple of chums.

'Bring them along – the more the merrier!' was the generous reply.

The brief opening ceremony duly completed, Kenneth and his pals were shown to their table, where they were joined by the governor, the admiral and their captain. Kenneth asked the latter the name of his ship, to which he answered the *Eagle*.

'Well, in that case you'll know Sylvester and James here,' Kenneth replied.

'There are more than 2,000 men under my command,' said the captain tartly. 'It's hardly likely that I should remember every face.'

'All the same,' began Kenneth, groping for something to fill an embarrassing gap in the conversation, 'as Dr Johnson says, "When it comes to lapidary inscriptions, no man is upon oath."'

'Very true,' said the captain uncertainly, 'very apt', and with that the conversation lurched off on to a different tack, fuelled by the timely arrival of fresh supplies of champagne.

A couple of drinks later a porter from Kenneth's hotel dashed in to say that the plane was finally ready to take off and that his luggage had been sent ahead to the airport. Bidding a hasty farewell to his companions, Kenneth was on his way out when the admiral asked what he was doing about transport. He said he'd get a taxi.

'Use my car,' boomed the admiral. And so it was that Kenneth arrived at Gibraltar airport, drove straight on to the tarmac and drew alongside the steps up to the plane in a huge Rolls-Royce flying the admiral's pennant.

The crew were lined up to welcome aboard their unexpected VIP, though their expressions altered somewhat when he emerged.

'It's only that twit from the *Carry Ons*,' said a steward, before asking Kenneth, 'I suppose you'll want a gin and tonic?' As he used to say, not even Dr Johnson would have had an answer to that.

Adolph Zukor was once the unknowing victim of a practical joke concocted by Buster Keaton and Fatty Arbuckle, who had just been signed up by Zukor to appear for Paramount. The setting chosen for this elaborate hoax was a dinner hosted by Arbuckle and served by Keaton as a ludicrously inept butler hired for the evening.

All the other guests had been warned in advance that the evening might be a trifle chaotic. Zukor was the only one kept in the dark.

The hors d'oeuvre of shrimps arrived without noticeable mishap, except that Keaton served the men before the women. This earned him a sharp rebuke from Arbuckle and, with muttered apologies, Keaton removed them from the men, in spite of several having been eaten, and placed them in front of the ladies.

After the shrimps came soup. At least that was what the guests were led to expect when the butler presented them with soup plates. However, a tremendous crash from the kitchen followed by further noises of broken crockery and glass led to uncertainty. Their worst fears were confirmed when Keaton reappeared, apparently saturated with soup, and solemnly removed the plates without explanation.

While all this was going on, Fatty Arbuckle was complaining volubly about the problems of finding reliable staff. In his view, the situation had deteriorated so drastically that he was seriously thinking of quitting the movies and leaving Hollywood altogether. To Adolph Zukor this was disastrous news.

Worse was to follow.

Bebe Daniels, seated beside her host, asked the butler for a glass of water. Mesmerized by her beauty Keaton stared helplessly into her eyes while pouring a jug of iced water into Arbuckle's lap. This was too much and, jumping to his feet, Arbuckle grabbed the wretched butler round the neck and would have throttled him if the other men at the table hadn't forcibly intervened. Buster Keaton slunk back into the kitchen while the guests tried to resurrect the conversation.

When the butler next appeared, he was carrying a magnificent turkey on a silver salver. So intent was he on bearing this safely to the table that he inadvertently let his napkin drop from his grasp. As he bent to pick this up a fellow accomplice in the kitchen flung open the swing door. In the best traditions of Hollywood slapstick, both turkey and butler were sent flying. The next few moments passed in an agony of horrified silence and awful anticipation as Keaton repeatedly failed to retrieve the turkey and Arbuckle approached boiling point. The two events coincided and just as Buster managed to get the turkey back on the salver, Fatty Arbuckle's fury exploded into a tirade of abuse and a hail of blows. His appalled guests saw him chase Keaton into the kitchen, whence came a cacophony of screams and crashes. The last they saw of the butler was his flight from the house with his erstwhile employer in hot and livid pursuit.

Fatty Arbuckle returned presently with the welcome news that he had a substitute turkey which could be prepared, if his guests wouldn't mind an intermission. After what they'd been through, a break from the dinner table was more than welcome.

While they were enjoying a relaxing drink, the phone rang and from Fatty Arbuckle's conversation they gathered that his friend Buster Keaton was on the line. In fact Arbuckle asked him to drop by and join his dinner party. (Buster had actually nipped upstairs, changed into his own clothes and telephoned down to Arbuckle on the internal telephone.)

When he arrived a short time later he was introduced to Adolph Zukor, who plainly didn't associate him with the butler who had so recently departed. It took several heavy hints from Arbuckle and the others before the penny dropped.

I have to confess to having been similarly duped. The setting was a dressing-room in Liverpool which I was sharing with Gerry Marsden when we were once appearing together in our home city. One evening Gerry had a visitor, an unprepossessing fellow whose mien wasn't helped by the fact that he was quite severely deformed by a humped back. Apparently he was a bosom pal of Gerry's from years back and was generously plied with drinks before Gerry went on stage. As soon as he was out of the room, however, this chap made a complete volte-face and began sounding off about his erstwhile friend in the most virulent and unpleasant way. But when Gerry rejoined us, his manner changed abruptly and he oozed fulsome praise for his friend, which I found a bit thick.

The next time Gerry went on stage exactly the same thing happened; if anything the so-called friend's abusive tirade became even worse. I was really seeing red by now and blew my top when Gerry got back, telling him that he ought to ask the fellow to leave before I punched him on the nose — or words to that effect. However, it was Gerry who did the punching. Accusing our visitor of all manner of treachery and guile, he laid into him furiously, thumping his hump and hurling him to the floor. I remember watching with horror as the fellow's false teeth flew out and he began whimpering pitifully. In the event I began to fear for his life and tried to pull Gerry off him.

That was the point when they both suddenly sat up grinning and I realized that the whole thing was a put up job and that Gerry's friend was no more a humpback than I am.

Set alongside the many triumphs of his career, Auguste Escoffier used to recall the appalling mishap of a newly engaged waiter entrusted with a bowl of peas who managed to tip its entire contents into the deep décolletage of one of the lady guests. He was so totally thrown by the enormity of what had happened that he began desperately to remove them one by one while muttering apologies in broken English, until he was sent reeling by a blow from the lady's equally appalled husband.

I enjoy the story told of the diner in a London restaurant famed for the quality of its food who asked for fish fingers when the waiter came to take his order.

'Birds Eye or Findus, sir?' inquired the waiter without the merest hint of reproof or surprise.

Finding one's favourite table occupied can be a trifle galling, I have to admit. How many of us, I wonder, would resolve the matter quite as tellingly as the newspaper magnate James Gordon Bennett did when he found others seated at his favourite table in a Monte Carlo restaurant? Bennett had become particularly attached to this restaurant because of the chef's unparalleled success with the otherwise humble mutton chop. In fact, he was so fond of the chops and the establishment that he forsook all other restaurants in Monte Carlo and dined there night after night. So when he found that his table had been given to others, he felt a bit miffed and called for the owner. Whereas most of us, I imagine, might mutter a few words of mild reproach along the lines of being loyal and devoted customers, Bennett didn't mess about. He told the owner to sell him the restaurant there and then and wrote him a cheque for $40,000 on the spot to clinch the deal!

Barely had the ink dried when the occupants of the new owner's table were asked to leave, in spite of being midway through their meal. The new proprietor took his seat, called for mutton chops and tucked in as usual.

When he departed, a sizeable and, under the circumstances generous tip, was left behind. He gave the restaurant back to its original owner.

In contrast to Mr Bennett, who always found what he wanted, the story is told of the less accomplished gourmet whose pretensions were in no way hampered by culinary expertise – or lack of it.

For reasons best known to himself, he regularly frequented a modest suburban restaurant in spite of constantly criticizing the food and sending unsolicited advice to the chef. His one passion seemed to be tripe – a dish which, curiously, never appeared on the menu. That was until the afternoon when the restaurant owner had an idea while enjoying his customary Turkish bath.

So excited was he by this that he forsook his massage and raced back to share the scheme with the chef. Their strategy agreed on, they hurried out to buy the ingredients for the favoured dish of tripe and managed to collect them all before the shops closed.

That evening the gourmet was greeted by a beaming owner, who informed him that he had finally taken his advice and engaged a new chef. Furthermore, he had asked the new man to prepare the dish he had talked of so often as a modest gesture of thanks for his patronage and guidance.

Tickled pink by this, the gourmet ordered a light hors d'oeuvre as a prelude to his speciality. With that finished, the tripe duly arrived, covered in a lovingly prepared sauce which he savoured appreciatively before tucking in. With only a brief pause to inform the owner that he had done the right thing in getting rid of a chef who didn't know the first thing about tripe, he polished off the lot and called for his bill with a triumphant flourish.

His attitude changed dramatically when this arrived. In place of a bill for the tripe was one for a flat sponge from the Turkish bath which, parboiled and camouflaged with sauce, he had just enthusiastically consumed.

Before President Jimmy Carter moved into the White House with his family as the thirty-ninth US president, his good lady was on the blower to the chef to check that he was familiar with the sort of Southern cuisine which the Carters were used to eating back home in Georgia.

'Yes, ma'am,' she was reassured to hear, 'we've been fixing that kind of food for the servants for a long time.'

Salvador Dali once took it into his head to go for a coffee in a New York restaurant accompanied by his pet ocelot, which he tied to a table leg while his order was brought.

'What's that?' exclaimed a woman passing by as she caught sight of the animal.

'Only a cat,' Dali told her scornfully. 'I've painted it with an op art design.'

Relieved at this and a little shamefaced by her

initial response, the woman peered closely at his pet and told Dali, 'That's fine now I see what it is. At first I thought it was a real ocelot.'

The great Austrian musician Fritz Kreisler was a man of many talents: virtuoso violinist, composer and, when the mood took him, after-dinner entertainer. At any event, that was his lot when he was engaged by a Manhattan millionaire and his wife to play for their guests one evening after a dinner party.

Unaccustomed to engagements of this sort, Kreisler suggested a fee of $10,000, which, to his surprise, was paid in advance without question. However, this left him with little option but to appear at the appointed time. Bearing in mind the unusual nature of the occasion, he arrived in 'black tie' rather than evening dress. His hostess spotted this and took him aside to explain clearly that he wouldn't be required to mingle with the guests when he had finished playing. Kreisler thanked her and added apologetically, 'Had I known that I was not expected to mix with the guests, I would of course have come for $3,000.'

In the course of a journey George II stopped at a wayside inn for a bite to eat. The landlord served him with an egg, for which he charged the right royal sum of a guinea.

'Eggs must be very scarce in these parts,' said the king as he paid his bill.

'No, sire,' the innkeeper corrected him. 'It is kings that are scarce.'

One of Harry Houdini's less endearing sleights of hand from the point of view of his friends was his facility for avoiding his share of a restaurant bill. However, on one occasion a magician friend succeeded in redressing the balance by a sleight of hand of his own. He had been lunching with Houdini and a group of other music hall artistes and, as the meal drew to a close, he offered to show Houdini a new trick.

'Put your hands on the table, palms down,' he said, and the great escapologist did as he was told.

The conjuror then filled two glasses with water and balanced one on the back of each of Houdini's hands.

'OK – let's see you get out of that without paying the check,' he said, as he and the rest of the party made a swift exit.

Giving instructions to his butler that he was not at home to a notorious bore whose visit he anticipated, Sir Winston Churchill added, 'And to convince him that I am not in, smoke one of my cigars when you open the door.'

When the *Queen Mary* was returned to civilian service at the end of the last war, a special effort was made to attract first-class passengers. To this end the owners made it known that passengers were encouraged to ask for whatever they liked in the dining-room, even if it did not appear on the already ample menu.

So it was that a Texan oil millionaire ordered rattlesnake steaks for four. Now, rattlesnake was one of the few commodities for which there had been little anticipated demand and an urgent conference took place behind the scenes with the captain before a solution was arrived at. At dinner that evening the Texan and his party were served with eels on a silver salver carried by two stewards shaking rattles.

Among the guests entertained by King Edward VII and Queen Alexandra at Buckingham Palace on one occasion was an Indian gentleman who devised a novel way of disposing of the inedible stalks of asparagus. He simply threw them over his shoulder.

Fortunately, King Edward was among the first to spot this and promptly did the same. The other guests copied him and the Indian gentleman left the palace at the end of the evening without the slightest hint that anything had been amiss.

Lady Wenlock, whose husband served as Governor of Madras in the 1890s, compensated for a little deafness by means of an ear trumpet shaped like an entrée dish. This led to a certain amount of confusion at times. Dining in Florence once, the attentive Italian aristocrat seated next to her filled it with a selection of vegetables. At a ball in England, she left it on a piano for a while and when at supper the Prince of Wales spoke to her through it, he was met with a face full of cigarette ends and cigar butts stubbed out by other male guests, who had mistaken it for an ashtray.

Poor service and disappointing fare generally leave a feeling of irritation, matched only by one's impotence in exacting adequate retribution. Just occasionally the opportunity to get your own back presents itself, though seldom as satisfyingly as in the case of a surveyor in Kent, who took exception to the ploughman's lunch he was served in a snack bar in Deal while on a visit to a nearby construction site. No self-respecting ploughman would have given a second glance to the morsels of desiccated wholemeal loaf and venerable Cheddar which accompanied his bill for £2.80 (service included). A request for fresh supplies was met with Olympian indifference by the proprietor and the surveyor left feeling – well, cheesed off.

A month later he had occasion to visit Deal again and, having half an hour to kill, returned to the snack bar, not to eat this time but to undertake a quick survey.

He timed his arrival to coincide with the lunch-time rush. Equipped with tape and clipboard and sporting his hard hat, he pushed his way through the throng of plainly less discerning customers, accompanied by a colleague whose aid had been enlisted in exchange for a pint of bitter when their mission was completed.

Together they began to measure the doorways and windows, the ceiling height and distance from wall to wall, while exchanging remarks like, 'We can drop the premix straight in if we come off the curb outside and take the glass out by next Tuesday. But make sure they don't leave it smashed all over the pavement like last time.'

Their measurements continued with references

to 'computer ducts' and 'steel doors' until interrupted by the proprietor's flustered demands to know what they were up to.

'Don't bother us just now,' said the surveyor curtly. 'We've got two more jobs to do and we're running late as it is.'

'What the hell do you mean?' retorted the snack bar owner. 'I run this place. What the heck do you think you're up to?'

'I'm only working from the plans,' was the answer. 'What plans?' asked the proprietor, fast losing his self-control.

'The ones for the alterations, of course.'

'Alterations? What alterations?!'

'Don't ask me. I'm just checking a few of the measurements before the lads move in next week,' said the surveyor, reeling in his tape and working his way through the queue of customers to the counter.

'Wait a minute,' exclaimed the owner. 'What about my lease?'

'Ask the landlord – not me,' said the surveyor, finishing behind the counter and pushing his way to the door, followed by his friend.

One final look back confirmed that was exactly what the proprietor was doing as he struggled towards the telephone, livid with rage.

It must be said in defence of all those who run the many estimable small establishments of this sort that for every proprietor cast in the mould described above, there is a legion of courteous and generous owners whose hospitality is always warm and whose sustenance seldom fails to satisfy. Here I can speak with a modicum of authority.

In the days before I donned my television cassock as the Rev Mervyn Noote or Brother Dominic's robe, I was invited to a fancy-dress party thrown by a photographer chum of mine, one Tom Hustler by name, in a basement in Mayfair. He had suggested that I should go as a tramp and I decided, somewhat unwisely as it turned out, to go as a Victorian clergyman, in battered top hat, dog collar, pinstripe trousers and spats.

It was a hot Sunday evening and I emerged from the lurid basement for a quick lungful of air and, as I was starting to feel peckish, a quick sandwich.

To my delight I saw a glimmer of light in an Italian café across the road and went over to state my needs: 'Excuse me, landlord, is there the slightest possibility of getting a cheese sandwich?'

'For you-a,' he said, 'no cheese sandwich. For you, the verra besta steaka.' And before I could say a word, the café was reopened and I was sitting down to a mouthwatering steak alla da trimmings.

'Is that your parish over there?' inquired my new-found friend, pointing to St George's Church in Hanover Square.

'No,' I replied quite openly. 'I'm St Philip's, in Kensington.' Which happened to be the case.

'And your name-a, pleze?'

'Nimmo,' said I, by now a little limp.

'Aah, Father Neemo, but you musta meeta my family before you go.' And down the stairs bounded a bevy of bambinos – Lucia, Anna, Maria, Sophia . . .

Sensing that things had already gone too far, I decided it was time for me to scarper. I hastened to pay my bill. But my money was waved aside. 'No, no, Father Neemo, no charge. Eet ees my pleasure.'

In desperation I plunged a crisp note into the Red Cross box that happened to be handily adjacent and made for the door. The noise wafting over the road from the party had now reached alarming proportions and it was obvious I could not rejoin it immediately. So, wishing the family, by now clustered all round me, a happy *buona notte*, I was forced to trudge several blocks before I felt the coast was sufficiently clear for me to hop back and rejoin the debauchery.

The steak proved to be something of a necessity after all.

A young woman who ordered steak and chips in a café was told by the waiter that unfortunately the steak was off that day.

'Then I'll have fish and chips,' she replied.

'The fish is off, too, I'm afraid.'

'Well, what have you got, then?'

'Only sausages, I'm afraid, madam.'

'OK, I'll have sausages and chips.'

More bad news was to follow – there were no chips either.

'Well, what do you have to go with the sausages?'

'Nothing, madam; only a few kind words.'

So the sausages were served and when the waiter inquired whether she wanted anything else, the woman replied with a smile, 'What about those kind words?'

'I wouldn't eat the sausages,' came the reply.

At one time an inn in Surrey carried the notice, 'A chef is available to barbecue T-bone steaks, beefburgers and sausages, with customers giving a hand if they wish.'

In later life Dame Edith Sitwell collected her room key in a hotel where she was staying and was asked by the porter, 'Anything in the morning, madam?' 'Only a coffin,' she replied mournfully.

'Will that be black or white, madam,' he replied.

Having had the pleasure and good fortune to dine in many restaurants around the globe, I have also greatly enjoyed the colourful and evocative English translations of local fare that can brighten and add a sense of true mystery to any meal.

A while ago *The Times* invited readers to send in some of their favourite menu entries following the discovery by its archaeological correspondent of '5 Apron Rice, Crab Meat Shaag and Botty Kebab' at the Sitara Restaurant in New York.

In response I offered a modest 'Claypot with eight fairies', which I had encountered in Bangkok. I was by no means alone in discoveries of this nature. From the Aegean island of Naxos came 'Lamb cook to a Peasant and Small Try'; Lady Kinloss reported coming across 'Fried Brian' in Granada; while the Turkish ship *Karadeniz* reportedly offered the somewhat ambivalent 'Farte aux fraises' to her passengers.

Be My Guest

As the recipient of much hospitality around the world, experience has taught me not to be surprised any more by what one encounters.

On a recent visit to Nigeria (the one that featured a slightly unnerving encounter with curried goat, or one particular part of the said beast, as mentioned elsewhere) I stayed at the splendid Hilton Hotel in Abuja – splendid both in its opulence and its isolation, because the Hilton appears to be just about the only building standing in the new federal capital currently under construction. The guards on the gate are decked out in full Hilton livery, as one might expect. Catch sight of them at night, though, and you'll find them carrying bows and arrows!

That experience was nothing compared with the 'Arabian night' I once had the misfortune to spend in a hotel in Tehran. In a way the Shah was to blame. He decided that the time had come to celebrate 2,000 years of monarchy in Persia (which was fraudulent in itself since his father had been only a colonel in the army). Nevertheless, crowned heads from around the world descended on the country, along with countless spectators who hadn't the faintest chance of sampling all those peacocks and Royal Iranian caviar – among whom I counted myself.

I hadn't had the opportunity to book a hotel in Tehran in advance and, arriving late in the evening, I set out to find somewhere to spend the night. As my Persian is somewhat limited, I had to explain in mime to an adjacent taxi driver that I was rather keen on finding an inn.

I have never been frightfully good at sign language. It often seems to land me in unexpected complications. Like the time I was trying to indicate to a lady chemist outside Barcelona that my wife, Pat, was suffering from constipation. I nearly got arrested for that one!

This time, however, I was fairly restrained and, having gone through a quick demonstration of getting undressed and lying on an imaginary bed, the Persian fellow cottoned on to the idea that I was looking for some spot to rest my weary head. He drove me to a disturbingly bleak establishment in what was quite clearly a particularly unfashionable part of town, and I was passed on to the proprietor – whom I took to be a kinsman of my cabby chum – and shown into my room.

The said proprietor opened the bedroom door, which was, curiously enough, next to his office, and switched on the light. The bulb seemed rather underendowed with watts, but even by its faint light it was fairly obvious that the furnishings were what even an unscrupulous estate agent could call only adequate: two single beds, one chair and a rather badly cracked and tapless washbasin. Furthermore, the room possessed an odour which suggested that it had been a popular resting-place for itinerant camel drivers.

I was just about to launch into another mime to the effect that I would seek accommodation elsewhere when the proprietor said something presumably cheery in Persian and was gone. I shouted after him with a rather lacklustre 'what-ho' and decided to make the best of a decidedly bad job. I personally have withstood the rigours of Boy Scout camps, British Rail sleeping-cars and the dressing-rooms of The Electric Theatre, Dumfries, without turning an occasional hair. But what I found most disturbing were the signs of recent occupation . . . an elderly toothbrush, a pair of particularly unsavoury old socks and a battered suitcase, the contents of which even wild horses would not have persuaded me to investigate.

Spreading a handy copy of the *Melbourne Sun* I had purloined from my Quantas jet on the solitary chair, I placed my jacket upon it. I then unfolded the Business Supplement and laid this on what would surely have been a Persian carpet, if there had been a carpet at all, and proceeded to disrobe. When I was finally down to my suntan, I spread the Sports Section and the Women's Page to form a path to the washbasin, where I rapidly attended to what is generally accepted to being next to Godliness.

A quick dab with the old towel and then, by deft use of the Situations Vacant and Houses to Let, I made my way to bed. The state of the sheets sent me scurrying back via the Sits Vac and Hses to Lt to the Bus Sup, where I had left my overnight bag.

I extracted a duty-free bottle of French eau de Cologne and squirted it everywhere. Then I went to sleep surprisingly quickly, but after about two hours I was awakened by the noise of footsteps on my newspaper. I froze.

The light was switched on and an elderly and rather portly Persian gentleman beamed down at me. He then proceeded to take off all his clothes and chuck them on top of mine. My only word of Persian was their noise for 'thank you', but I thought I had far better be sociable and utter it as I didn't want to stand, or lie, aloof. He was soon tucked up in his bed and after contemplating for a few moments the chances of attempting a moonlight flit, I dozed off as well.

When I looked up in the morning, he was gone, and I never saw him again. What intrigues me is whether he just casually wandered in from the street or whether he was the proud owner of the battered suitcase and the grotty socks.

This was certainly much more of an adventure than all the champagne, caviar and silken four-poster coverings the Shah's lot got.

Quite the most extraordinary place where I have ever been the happy guest of gracious hosts was an extinct open mine in the Australian outback at a place called White Cliff. I was leaving Melbourne, having played in a season there, when a chum of mine offered the tantalizing proposition, 'Look, Derek, before you go, you've got to see the arsehole of Australia – White Cliff.'

How could I refuse?

So we rustled up three little aircraft and set off for White Cliff. As I was refuelling my plane at Broken Hill, the engineer asked where I was heading.

'White Cliff', I replied cheerily.

'White Cliff?' was his incredulous reply. 'Have you ever been to anywhere like White Cliff before?'

'Well, I've been to Tennant Creek,' I answered defensively.

'Compared with White Cliff, Tennant Creek's like Paris,' he said, and bid me what I considered an all-too-knowing farewell.

As we approached our destination, there appeared little pockmarks in the ground beneath, where all the open mines had been. Now, whereas in Europe we have spent generations getting out of caves, in White Cliff they've gone back into them – they're all troglodytes living underground. The only building above ground was the so-called White Cliff Hilton, which had beds that would have credited my room in Tehran and fly screens that had long since passed from useful service.

I had flown up with a frightfully nice couple whose daughter and boyfriend had removed themselves from the rat race and chosen to settle down in this extraordinary place. They were in the process of enlarging their cave and, while the work was in progress, their guests were accommodated on the surface in an old London double-decker bus. Not wishing to let down their Tuareg standards, they decided to have a cocktail party. So it was that at about seven-thirty, as the blazing heat of the day subsided, all their guests emerged from their holes to gather for drinks, while the girl's mother handed round plates of smoked oysters and other little canapés and we all drank champagne as the stars came out.

❋

Here is Mrs Beeton with a word or two of advice on the subject of hospitality:

> Hospitality is a most excellent virtue, but care has to be taken that the love of company for its own sake does not become a prevailing passion, for then the habit is no longer hospitality, but dissipation. Reality and truthfulness in this, as in all other duties of life, are the points to be studied for, as Washington Irving well says: 'There is an emanation from the heart in genuine hospitality which cannot be described, but is immediately felt, and puts the stranger at once at his ease.' With respect to the continuance of friendships, however, it may be found necessary in some cases for the mistress to relinquish, on assuming the responsibility of a household, many of those commenced in the earlier part of her life. This will be the more requisite if the number still retained be quite equal to her means and opportunities.

In contrast to the exquisite meals enjoyed by James Bond and described in mouthwatering detail in his novels, the food served at Ian Fleming's own table in Jamaica was known to be both sparse and virtually inedible. Noël Coward once described a meal there as tasting like armpits. On another occasion a guest who fancied he had been served with toad-in-the-hole went to scoop a couple of sausages from the glass dish and found that they wriggled away as his spoon touched them. The plump, inviting sausages turned out to be the fingers of his host's servant waiting at table.

When George Neville was installed as Archbishop of York in 1464, 600 guests attended the celebratory feast. Among the culinary delights provided were: 300 quarters of wheat, 300 tuns of ale, 100 tuns of wine, one pipe of hippocras, 104 oxen, six wild bulls, 1,000 sheep, 304 calves, 304 'porkes', 400 swans, 2,000 geese, 1,000 capons, 2,000 pigs, 104 peacocks. In addition there were more than 135,000 fowl of different kinds, in excess of 500 deer, over 600 freshwater fish, a dozen porpoises and seals, 1,500 venison pasties and 13,000 jellies, tarts and custards.

During one of Grover Cleveland's two terms as US president he and Mrs Cleveland entertained a number of foreign diplomats at the White House to dinner one evening. On the guest list was a young European attaché, who noticed a worm on the salad with which he had been served. Just as he was about to call back the waiter, he saw the president's wife glaring at him. Without a word he cleared his plate, worm and all.

'You will go far, young man,' said a smiling Mrs Cleveland. She was right. Fifteen years later her guest returned to Washington as his country's ambassador.

Calvin Coolidge, an American president as taciturn as others have been prolix, once entertained a newly arrived British ambassador to Washington. When they had been served coffee the president poured a little cream into a saucer. His guest politely did the same. Seeing this, Coolidge smiled and then without comment bent down and put the saucer of cream in front of the cat sitting patiently beneath the table at his feet.

At one dinner party given by Theodore Roosevelt Nancy Astor was given precedence in the seating-plan over Grace Vanderbilt. Anxious to dispel any possible offence, she confided to Mrs Vanderbilt, 'The Astors skinned skunks 100 years before the Vanderbilts worked ferries.'

The other Roosevelt to take up residence in the White House, Franklin D, once tried a little experiment based on something he had read to the effect that guests seldom bother to listen to the greetings or farewells offered by their hosts since they are usually thinking of what to say themselves.

Putting this to the test, the president greeted each guest with his famous smile and the cheerful comment, 'I murdered my grandmother this morning.' Apparently no one batted an eyelid except for a prominent Wall Street broker, who replied to the president's words of welcome, 'She certainly had it coming.'

At the end of one of Lord Lonsdale's dinner parties an eastern diplomat who had been present made his farewells and told his lordship, 'I must not cockroach on your time any longer.'

Seeing him to the door the earl congratulated his guest on his rapid command of English and hoped he wouldn't be offended if he pointed out one tiny solecism – that the word he meant to use was 'encroach' not 'cockroach'.

'Forgive me,' said the oriental gentleman. 'I was addressing you personally and therefore used "cockroach". If I had been addressing her ladyship, then I would certainly have used the feminine "hencroach".'

❋

One might imagine that to be the sole guest of six hosts is an unexpected honour. Indeed, that was the response of the nineteenth-century Liberal statesman Sir William Harcourt, who was once invited to dine with half-a-dozen gentlemen, each of whom had taken the trouble to write to him personally. So touched was he by this gesture that he took the incautious step of inquiring why he should have been singled out for this special distinction. Some questions are better left unasked and this was one of them.

His hosts, it appeared, had each arranged to invite as his guest the man he considered to be the most unpopular in London.

A guest invited to a country house arrived to find the place engulfed in flames and his hostess striding up and down the terrace, urging on the firemen. 'I say,' he asked her, not wishing to show his surprise, 'you did say this evening, didn't you?'

A guest at Woburn was asked by the Duke of Bedford what she thought of the beautiful Canalettos in the dining-room. The lady replied that she loved them, especially with cheese.

Count D'Orsay, hailed as 'the last of the dandies', was dining with Benjamin Disraeli in Downing Street at a meal in which everything was served too cold. That was until the ices made their appearance, melting and slopping in their dishes.

'At last we have something hot,' exclaimed the Count.

Good Queen Bess was in the habit of dropping in on her wealthier subjects, accompanied by her entire court and staying for several weeks. This brought several of them close to the brink of financial ruin and acted as a subtle way of maintaining her upper hand in the country.

Few of her subjects 'chosen' to receive this honour complained when the royal entourage hove into view. One who did mutter a word of dissent was Sir Nicholas Bacon, her Lord Keeper of the Great Seal, who was told by the Queen on her arrival, 'My Lord Bacon, what a little house you've gotten.'

In reply, Bacon said to the Queen, 'Madam, my house is well, but it is your Highness that has made me too great for my house.'

The coronation of Edward VII in 1901 had a couple of unexpected elements. For one thing the king was taken ill and the coronation had to be postponed at two days' notice while the royal appendix was removed. As a consequence, many of London's poor feasted on the 2,500 quails and hundreds of partridges, chickens and sturgeon that had been prepared for the coronation banquet.

Then there was the matter of a few hundred invitations which mysteriously surfaced among the richest citizens of Chicago. Bearing the royal coat of arms and printed on fine linen stationery, these carried an unusual wording which the recipients would have done well to read carefully before rushing for their glad rags and jumping on the first ship bound for these shores. These were the instructions:

Those honoured with invitations to the coronation are expected to give particular attention to their attire, and must be clothed according to rank. Peers and peeresses of the realm, baronets, knights and ladies, and members of the gentry are privileged to wear the royal crimson velvet, with coronets, tiaras, necklaces, rings, ear-rings, bracelets, epaulets, buckles, collarettes, sashes embroidered with strawberry leaves in gilt, girdles, stomachers, silver gilt crowns, and capes edged with twenty-five rows of minever. Titled nobility from America, such as merchant princes, coal barons, trust magnates, lords of finance with their ladies, must appear in costumes typifying the origins of their titles, and they may carry tape measures, coal scuttles, oil cans, stock tickers, and other heraldic devices, and may wear stick pins, clothes pins, scarf pins, coupling pins, hair pins, rolling pins, cuff buttons, shoe strings, picture hats, turbans, handcuffs, overcoats, imitation lace scarfs, celluloid collars, hose or half hose as the case may be, rhinestones, collar buttons of silver gilt, and golf capes edged with two and one-half rows of rabbit skin.

By special royal proclamation it is commanded and decreed that during and after the coronation when healths and toasts are to be drunk or thirsts are to be quenched either in high-balls, cocktails, sours, or any other mixed drinks also by means of whiskey straights; old underhoof rye, manufactured by Chas Dennehy & Co, of Chicago, USA, shall be used, as it has been found by His Majesty to be the very best, purest and most ancient whiskey vended.

By order of THE EARL MARSHALL

Invited to a shoot once, Edward VII was adamant that the only guests at luncheon should be the guns and their ladies. However, his hostess could not restrain herself from broadcasting her social coup and dispatched invitations considerably beyond this limit.

The extended party did not escape His Majesty's eye and, as they gathered for lunch, he made a point of telling her, 'I see that you have appointed the *monde*.'

'Only the demimonde, Your Majesty,' was her unthinking reply.

In her youth Lady Diana Cooper was invited to dinner at the viceregal lodge in Dublin. On arrival the viceroy's wife, Lady Wimborne, took her aside and confided, 'I must warn you, dearest Diana, that in curtseying to His Excellency after dinner, we don't use the gavotte or Court curtsey, but rather the modern Spanish.'

The young guest replied that His Excellency would have to make do with whatever bob he could get from her, 'plus hiccups if it's after dinner'.

There is a delightful story told of the wedding reception held to celebrate the marriage of the then Princess Royal to the sixth Earl of Harewood. E M Forster, portly and alarmingly short-sighted, was among the guests and was seen at one point bowing with great dignity to the wedding cake in the mistaken belief that it was Queen Mary.

❋

Not many years later Lord Tyrrell was appointed British ambassador in Paris and took up residence in the Embassy, where he was occasionally joined by his wife. Lady Tyrrell's interests did not altogether follow a parallel course to those commonly associated with the wives of our diplomats. At the time she was engrossed in writing a history of the world, a work of truly global proportions that sought to trace the development of civilization right around the world from the second millennium BC to the present day. Research for this necessarily kept her away from Paris for long periods and, when she was in residence, she spent most of her time sitting in a tree in the Embassy gardens, writing away.

Occasionally, she descended to join her husband in official receptions, where rather surprisingly her charm, good humour and habitual vagueness made her a great hit. The latter not infrequently resulted in interesting, if slightly baffling, encounters for her guests. At dinner one evening she spent an hour or so talking to F E Smith (Lord Birkenhead) under the misapprehension that he was the Turkish ambassador, while the Duke of York (later to become King George V) was mistaken for Lord Tyrrell's private secretary.

Rules are rules and in London's older clubs they have been rules for a very long time. One club, for instance, does not permit visitors into the lounge – and there are no exceptions. So it was that Her Majesty the Queen, invited to a private dinner party and nipping into the lounge to admire the pictures, had to be called back by Prince Philip, hissing, 'Not in there, Bet.'

This disturbed an elderly member of the club, who raised himself from his doze, caught sight of his departing monarch and grumbled, 'Who was that woman? What's she doing here?'

'That was the Queen, my lord,' answered a waiter.

'Well, dammit, she shouldn't be here,' the old fellow retorted. 'Members only, you know.'

As the Head of the Commonwealth, Her Majesty the Queen has always enjoyed entertaining visiting heads of state. Sir Robert Menzies attended a dinner at Buckingham Palace at which Sir Winston Churchill and the Muslim prime minister of Pakistan were also among the guests and recorded a snippet of their conversation after dinner. As Her Majesty's prime minister, Churchill took upon himself the duties of host and inquired, 'Will you have a whisky and soda, Mr Prime Minister?'

'No, thank you!' was the firm reply.

'What's that?'

'No, thank you.'

'What, why?'

'I'm a teetotaller, Mr Prime Minister.'

'A teetotaller. Christ! I mean God! I mean Allah!'

According to Sir Robert Menzies, there was then a general stampede to relate this story to the Queen. He thought he had beaten the rest, but he had been pipped at the post. 'You're too late. Tommy Lascelles has told me about it,' said the Queen, 'and Tommy says that as the footman, in his astonishment, dropped the tray and caught it before it reached the carpet, without spilling a drop, he ought to be put into the English cricket team, where the slip-fielding needs improving.'

It was at another Commonwealth gathering presided over by Churchill that word reached him surreptitiously during the meal that one of the distinguished guests had been spotted pocketing a silver salt shaker. Churchill immediately slipped a matching pepper shaker into his own pocket. At the end of the meal he approached the offending guest guiltily and said, 'I'm afraid we were seen. Perhaps we had better put them back.'

Not all royal entertaining takes the form of lavish official banquets. Peter Hall was among the 800 guests invited to the party given at Buckingham Palace to celebrate the Queen's Jubilee in the summer of 1977. He described a relaxed, easy-going affair, with the Royal Family mixing informally with their guests – very informally in Peter Hall's case. Escaping from the throng gathered around the breakfast table at one in the morning, his hands filled with three plates of sausages and scrambled eggs and a cigar in his mouth, he bumped into the Duke of Edinburgh, who started chatting to him. Sir Peter's temporary indisposition was relieved by a footman, who thoughtfully took the cigar from his mouth so that he could reply.

The extraordinary story is told of an invitation to dinner that Hermann Goering sent to the singer Josephine Baker during the last war. Knowing that the American dancer and singer was married to a Jewish businessman and worked with the Resistance, Goering and the Gestapo decided to murder her by putting cyanide in her fish.

Miss Baker was warned of this threat and excused herself as the fish course was served, hoping to make her escape down the laundry chute in the bathroom. However, Goering drew his pistol and commanded her to eat the fish before letting her leave the room. She managed to make it to the bathroom and down the chute, where fellow members of the Resistance whisked her away to a doctor, who pumped out her stomach and saved her life. It took her a month to recover, but that dinner party cost her all her hair and from then on she had to wear a wig.

The French novelist and playwright Tristran Bernard was taking tea one afternoon with a lady whose stinginess knew few bounds. Offered a plate of rum babas, he noticed that they had been cut in two. 'Thank you, madame,' he said, helping himself. 'I will have a ba.'

On another occasion he had been invited to dine with a hostess whose generosity and the quality of whose cuisine was the exact opposite. So it struck her as slightly odd that an hour after the time of arrival Bernard had still not shown up. Worried that something may have happened to him, she telephoned, only to be told by the novelist that he wasn't coming.

'Not coming?'

'No,' he replied. 'I'm not hungry.'

Alfred Hitchcock was another trencherman who took a low view of sparsely provisioned meals. Towards the end of a dinner party where the portions fell some way short of his expectations, Hitchcock's host remarked, 'I do hope you will dine with us again soon.'

'By all means,' said the master of suspense. 'Let's start now.'

Economy was the watchword by which Venetia James exercised her unique talent as a hostess. In spite of being born a Cavendish-Bentinck and marrying an American millionaire, she was habitually conscious of waste, especially where domestic economy was concerned. Tradesmen became used to dealing with her household at Coton in Northamptonshire on a sale-or-return basis, of which the latter contributed a significant amount to the domestic budget, thanks to Mrs James's extreme care when feeding her guests. On one occasion she arranged for a chicken to be carved in such a way that it served ten – a triumph that enabled her to slip a note to the butler reading DCSC (Don't Carve Second Chicken).

Not that she was enthusiastic about the serving of any meat. Fish, which was cheaper, always took precedence in her scale of economy and not infrequently led to her audible whispers when Catholic guests were dining, 'Fish for the Papists! Fish for the Papists!'

❃

During the thirty-two years that he was Master of Trinity College, Cambridge, Dr Henry Butler used to invite freshmen to breakfast with him as a way of getting to know them and introducing them to the civilizing influence of a Cambridge education. One morning he entered the breakfast room and was greeted by a group of anxious young faces. Glancing out of the window he sought to break the ice by commenting, 'Well, we have a little sun this morning.'

This remark prompted one of his shy guests to inquire, 'I do hope that Mrs Butler is doing well, Master.'

The story is told that Warden Spooner of New College, Oxford, he of the eponymous Spooner-ism, once accidentally upset a saltcellar on a clean linen tablecloth. Reaching for his wine glass, he immediately sprinkled a few drops of claret on to the spilled salt.

The poet Samuel Rogers, better remembered to-day, I suspect, for his *Table Talk*, invited Lord Byron to dinner one evening and recalled the event as follows:

When we sat down to dinner I asked Byron if he would take soup? 'No, he never took soup.' Would he take some fish? 'No, he never took fish.' Presently I asked if he would eat some mutton? 'No, he never ate mutton.' – I then asked if he would take a glass of wine? 'No, he never tasted wine.' It was now necessary to inquire what he did eat and drink; and the answer was, 'Nothing but hard biscuits and soda water.' Unfortunately neither hard biscuits nor soda water were at hand; and he dined upon potatoes bruised down on his plate and drenched with vinegar. – My guests stayed till very late discussing the merits of Walter Scott and Joanna Baillie. – Some days after, meeting Byron's friend Hobhouse, I said to him, 'How long will Lord Byron persevere in his present diet?' He replied, 'Just as long as you continue to notice it.' I did not then know what I now know to be a fact – that Byron, after leaving my house, had gone to a club in St James's Street, and eaten a hearty meat supper.

Alexandre Dumas the elder told the story of a politician who received two huge sturgeon as a present and was slightly exercised as to how to make the best social capital out of his windfall. In consultation with his chef he went through the various options. They agreed that serving both at dinner would easily be taken as a sign of extravagance and poor taste. On the other hand, serving one fish at dinner and the other at luncheon the following day would understandably be a trifle tedious and would rob the politician of the chance to show off his munificence.

In the end they struck on the perfect solution. When the time came for the main course to be served that evening, the dining-room was filled with music as flautists and fiddlers led in a procession of torch-bearing footmen who heralded the arrival the smaller of the sturgeon, borne aloft on a bed of roses. However, disaster struck just as it was about to be placed on the table. One of the chefs appeared to stumble and the magnificent fish slid to the floor. The guests were aghast. Savouring the moment for as long as he dared, their host relished their obvious disappointment before commanding imperiously, 'Serve the other!'

The inventor Thomas Alva Edison had little time for formal dinners and, finding himself at one such function surrounded by people with whom he had nothing in common, resolved to escape as soon as seemed decently fit. But as he was inching towards the door, he was collared by his host, who said, 'I'm so pleased you were able to come, Mr Edison. Tell me, what are you working on now?'

'My exit,' replied the inventor.

❄

In 1757 Frederick the Great won one of his most celebrated victories, at the Battle of Rossbach, leading his Prussian army to an overwhelming defeat of the combined French and German forces. The enemy suffered heavy losses and many French officers were captured. In the best traditions of chivalrous warfare, Frederick invited them to dine with him. Apologizing for the rather restricted fare on offer, he explained, 'But, gentlemen, I did not expect you so soon and in such large numbers.'

One of London's most famous hostesses of the 1920s was Mrs Ronald Greville, heiress to the McEwan brewing fortune. Ever conscious of her position, she did not take kindly to other women who sported jewellery more eye-catching than her own. At dinner once she was confronted by an American lady every bit as wealthy as herself and festooned with a magnificent diamond necklace. As the party were rising from the table the American lady suddenly realized that she had lost her principal stone, which sent everyone scurrying round on their hands and knees to find it – all, that is, except for Mrs Greville. She was overheard remarking, 'Perhaps this might be of some assistance', as she handed a footman a large magnifying-glass.

❋

For all her confidence on the printed page, Mrs Beeton acknowledged that for a hostess the lead-up to a dinner party could be quite an ordeal. As always, she had words of advice and comfort suited to the occasion:

> The half-hour before dinner is the great ordeal through which the mistress, in giving a dinner party, will either pass with flying colours, or lose many of her laurels. The anxiety to receive her guests – her hope that all will be present in due time – her trust in the skill of her cook and the attention of the other domestics, all tend to make the few minutes a trying time. The mistress, however, must display no kind of agitation, but show her tact in suggesting light and cheerful subjects of conversation which will be much aided by the introduction of any particularly new book, curiosity of art or article of virtue which may pleasantly engage the attention of the company. Photograph albums, crest albums, new music will aid to pass a few moments pleasantly.

The artist Walter Sickert entertained a couple of young men to tea in his studio one afternoon and found time hanging rather heavily on his hands as they accepted further refreshment and made no obvious signs of imminent departure. When they finally got up to thank him and say goodbye,

Sickert replied cheerfully, 'Do come back, when you've a little less time to spare.'

A guest who had similarly outstayed his welcome eventually rose to leave and thanked his host and hostess, saying, 'I did enjoy myself. I hope I haven't kept you up too late.'

'Not at all,' replied the husband. 'We should have been getting up soon anyway.'

Party-giving at home did not always agree with P G Wodehouse. His wife, Ethel, relished any opportunity to entertain but Plum was a touch more reticent. A few guests arriving slightly after everyone else at one of her do's rang the door bell and found Plum opening it in place of the butler. Recognizing the new arrivals as friends, he held up the palms of his hands as if to push them away and said, 'Don't come. You'll hate it!'

Having for many years suffered jibes both good- and ill-natured about his name, a certain Mr Pierce-Bottom decided to exact a small amount of personal satisfaction from his unfortunate predicament. Unable to do much about his name, he decided that others might just as well share his lot.

Combing through telephone directories he soon compiled a list of the similarly afflicted: Bottomleys, Bottoms, Greenbottoms, Higginbottoms, Sidebottoms and Winterbottoms. These soon became the recipients of invitations to an exclusive dinner in London. Pierce-Bottom chose the basement of a hotel for his gathering and selected rump steak for the menu. A good many of those invited turned up for the event, though only one 'bottom' derived any pleasure from the evening. That was Pierce-Bottom himself, who had stayed comfortably at home, leaving each of his 'guests' to pay their own bill.

Guests at a luncheon held by the Welsh Arts Council Sculpture Committee some fifteen years ago were tolerably surprised to be served their meal on crockery that bore an alarming resemblance to parts of the human anatomy – the female one. The body in question was that of the sculptor Beryl Cheame, who seemingly hit on the idea of moulding this novel dinner service around herself, so to speak, during a dinner party. As she explained blithely, 'My breasts did for the soup bowls and my tummy for the plates. Later I added a casserole which was formed around a cast of my behind.'

One can only speculate on the nature of the conversation during which the inspiration came to her.

To be invited to stay as the guest of George Mathew at his home, Thomastown Castle, in County Tipperary, was to be indulged and pampered in a way unprecedented in any other private house in eighteenth-century Britain.

The only rule guests were asked to obey was that they should not acknowledge their bountiful host, treating him merely as a fellow guest. That understood, they were free to order whatever they chose for dinner and were given a free run in the castle's superbly stocked cellars.

Those who enjoyed tavern or coffee-house life were catered for by carefully created replicas of both, where staff were on hand at all hours to provide sustenance in keeping with both types of establishment.

Jonathan Swift was invited to Thomastown in 1719 for a fortnight and agreed to go only with some misgiving. In spite of receiving his hosts's traditional greeting – 'This is your castle. Here you are to command as absolutely as in your own home.' - he remained highly sceptical and ate in his own room for four days. Finding Mathew as good as his word, however, and perhaps beginning to miss the company of others, Swift ventured forth to dinner on the fifth night and enjoyed himself so completely that his two weeks at Thomastown turned effortlessly into sixteen!

'For what we are about to receive, and for what Mr Jones has already received, may the Lord make us truly thankful. Amen', runs one admonishing grace.

Gourmands and Gourmets

As may be evident, I do tend to fancy myself as a gastronome and bon vivant, so the visit I made some twenty years ago to what was laughingly known as a health hydro is an experience still vividly etched in my memory.

The savage sentence was imposed on me by my loving wife. Her reasoning ran along the lines that:

1 She said she was tired and needed a rest.
2 I had put on six pounds since Christmas.
3 If I was going away to have a holiday on my own, she thought I would be less likely to get into mischief if I were incarcerated in a health farm.

What I hadn't realized when agreeing to this enforced isolation was that my seven days wouldn't be that far a cry from those spent by Ivan Denisovich in Alexander Solzhenitsyn's merry tale about life in the gulag. (Coincidentally, he won the Nobel Prize for Literature at around the same time that I was incarcerated.)

The reality of life down on the farm came as a rude awakening. Early morning porridge drenched in brown sugar and cream, which I had hitherto enjoyed before settling down to toast and marmalade, before nibbling my way through the odd rasher of bacon, one or two stray tomatoes, a brace of bangers and, perchance, a generous portion of devilled kidneys, was cruelly swept aside to be substituted (if that is the word) by hot water and a slice of lemon.

The same ingredients constituted lunch.

Tea was simply tea.

Supper (and this was the big one!) amounted to four grapes and an orange.

If that wasn't enough to finish off body and soul, the former was then subjected to a variety of demanding pursuits. Soon after dawn I was pummelled by a masseur who, I am sure, would have had tremendous success in the Spanish Inquisition. Indeed, so fierce was his technique that I spent the last half of my stay having infra-red treatment to try and heal the bruises.

The rest of the time I divided between sitting stark naked in a sauna bath, sweltering at a temperature five degrees above boiling-point, and running through the grounds in my bare toes, weak and stumbling from hunger.

My only moment of excitement in the entire week was when one day I put my hand into my dressing-gown pocket and found a long-forgotten toffee.

After the first few days the hunger was absolutely frightful and the perils involved in trying to satisfy one's cravings were indeed manifold. If one was caught stuffing in the village tuckshop, expulsion was automatic!

But Nimmo, true to tradition, stuck to the rules

of the game throughout, even when faced with the unexpected temptation of opening a small parcel that his elder son, Timothy, had sent through the post. Horrid boy – it was a Mars Bar. Far from helping me to 'work, rest and play', it brought on an agony of conscience as I was tempted almost beyond endurance before hurling it unopened into the adjacent shrubbery.

I suspect I owe my survival to the relief that came in the form of Godfrey Evans, the renowned England wicketkeeper, who was particularly well known for his very bright-red gloves. He kept a pub just outside the gates of my establishment and as I was sitting mournfully in there on one of my seven days, he whispered, 'Derek, would you like a glass of Moët? I always keep a few half-bottles on ice for the inmates.' From then on I used to emerge from the sauna and slip down to Godfrey's tavern, there to receive a reviving glass of champagne from his ever-trusty hands.

When I emerged seven pounds lighter, limp and weak I headed straight for the nearest restaurant, there to indulge myself in the most enormous, fattening, calorie-ridden, butter-oozing meal of my tiny life.

From then on I vowed that others could eat an apple a day, suck a lemon or even blow a raspberry for all I cared. For me it was to be *bon appetit* all the way – and that was no sour grapes.

Well – it was twenty years ago and, while I may have softened my resolve just a little, the principle still holds true. The nearest I come to raw lemons these days is dropping generous slices of them into well-primed gins and tonics.

Bishop Samuel Wilberforce was fond of telling guests of the clergyman whose devotion to his own table was as great as that he showed to the Lord's. Whenever he was asked to say grace, he would scan the table for champagne glasses. If they were present, he would begin his grace, 'O most bountiful Jehovah...'; but if his eye met nothing grander than claret glasses, he would intone, 'We are not worthy, O Lord, of these, the least of Thy mercies...'

The Rev James Woodforde was an eighteenth-century parson whose devotion to the table left little room for the self-denial practised at other times by men of the cloth. His diary is filled with detailed accounts of colossal meals that would send any disciple of *cuisine naturelle* into apoplexy. Here is Parson Woodforde's account of 'a very elegant dinner' he enjoyed in Christ Church, Oxford, in 1774:

The first course was, part of a large cod, a chine of mutton, some soup, a chicken pye, pudding and roots, etc. Second course, pidgeons and asparagus, a fillet of veal with mushrooms and a high sauce with it, roasted sweetbreads, hot lobster, apricot tart and in the middle a pyramid of syllabubs and jellies. We had a dessert of fruit after dinner, and Madeira, White Port, and red to drink as wine. We were all very cheerful and merry.

❋

Kenneth Williams once worked with an actor at Birmingham Rep who was obsessed with food and always managed to turn any discussion round to his pet topic. In the course of conversation one day he told Kenneth, 'I popped over to see the Redgraves and we had a strawberry on the lawn.' As Kenneth said, he made it sound like intercourse.

Freddie Treves knew this chap too and, during a chat about the war, he inquired, 'Weren't you in the Navy?' The actor said that he had been and gave Freddie the name of his ship, which Freddie dimly remembered had been sunk.

'I was on her when she went down,' said his friend. 'We were picked up by a French corvette and we had the most wonderful *omelettes aux fines herbes* on board.'

That was his overriding memory of the whole ghastly incident.

The brilliant French farceur Georges Feydeau ordered lobster one day and was served with a crustacean that had lost one claw. When he pointed this out to the waiter, he was told that lobsters occasionally fought each other in the tank, causing these mishaps. Feydeau was not impressed. 'Take this one away,' he commanded, 'and bring me the victor.'

In 1856, the year that saw the end of the Crimean War, the first extraction of cocaine in its impure form and the beginning of Louis Pasteur's work into bacteriology, Eliza Acton published her *Modern Cookery for Private Families*, which had these handy hints on oysters that no 'private family' could surely do without:

The old-fashioned plan of *feeding* oysters with a sprinkling of oatmeal or flour, in addition to the salt and water to which they were committed, has long been rejected by all genuine amateurs of these nutritious and excellent fish, who consider the plumpness which the oysters are supposed to gain from the process, but poor compensation for the flavour which they are sure to lose. To cleanse them when they first come up from the beds, and to keep them in good condition for four or five days, they only require to be covered in cold water, with five ounces of salt to the gallon dissolved in it before it is poured on them; this should be changed with regularity every twenty-four hours. By following this plan with exactness they may be kept alive from a week to ten days, but will remain in perfect condition scarcely more than half that time. Oysters should be eaten always the instant they are opened. Abroad they are served before the soup in the first course of a dinner, arranged usually in as many plates as there guests at table. In England they are sometimes served *after* the soup. A sense of appropriateness must determine how far the variations of fashion should be followed in such matters.

❈

Not that many years ago four turtles, each weighing two hundredweight, were flown from Trinidad to London to act as the principal ingredients in the soup to be served at the Lord Mayor's Banquet. On arrival each turtle was given half-a-dozen oysters and a bottle of vintage champagne. A spokesman for the catering firm charged with preparing the soup explained that the champagne warmed and cheered the turtles – as well it might.

In an unexpected gesture of *entente cordiale* in the spring of 1958 Her Majesty the Queen received by post a tureen of tripe from a cook in France. Mind you, this was no ordinary tripe and no ordinary cook.

Prepared *à la mode de Caen*, the tripe was one of the specialities of a restaurateur who had been a founder member of the august fraternity of La Triperie d'Or.

In a letter of thanks from the British Embassy in Paris conveying royal thanks, he was told that the receipt of the tripe 'gave much pleasure to Prince Philip and Her Majesty the Queen, who were very touched the friendliness of your gesture'.

No mention was made as to whether the royal couple had actually sampled the celebrated Normandy dish, but the Embassy letter ended with words of congratulations to the restaurateur on the excellence of his cooking.

❋

At the end of the fourteenth century a treatise on 'home economics' entitled *Le Ménagier de Paris* laid down the basic requirements each week for all the royal courts. These included 496 sheep, seventy cattle, seventy calves, sixty-three hogs, seventeen salt hogs, 1,511 goats, 14,900 chickens, 12,390 pigeons and 1,511 goslings.

Quantities such as these reflect the fact that medieval monarchs were expected to show hospitality in due measure to the power they wielded. For this reason, if no other, Richard II apparently entertained 10,000 of his subjects every day!

As both Prince Regent and King, George IV's gargantuan excesses rivalled those of any British monarch before or since. His coronation cost an estimated £238,000, a substantial share of which went on the splendid banquet held in Westminster Hall. Five years earlier, in 1815, he engaged, at ruinous expense to his exchequer and his constitution, the services of Carème, the most celebrated chef of his day. While Carème claimed that during his two years' service the Prince Regent never suffered from gout, which his previously highly spiced diet had inflicted on him almost permanently, his cuisine had other side effects. The Prince commented on one occasion that 'dinner last night was superb, but you will make me die of indigestion', which brought from Carème the reply, 'Prince, my duty is to tempt your appetite, not to control it.'

However, two years of British weather and the British diet were enough for the master chef, who packed his bags and headed for the Russian court at St Petersburg, though not before penning these sardonic notes on English cooking, the essentials of which he wrote, 'are the roasts of beef, mutton, and lamb; the various meats cooked in salt water in the manner of fish and vegetables ... fruit preserves, puddings of all kinds, chicken and turkey with cauliflower, salt beef, country ham, and several similar ragouts – that is the sum of English cooking'. And so it remained for a good century and a half.

Carème's departure had little effect on the Prince's appetite. Even when he was seriously ill, he still managed to polish off a staggering amount of food and drink, as the Duke of Wellington recorded sourly in the spring of 1830:

What do you think of his breakfast yesterday morning for an invalid? A pigeon and beef steak pie of which he ate two pigeons and three beef steaks, three parts of a bottle of Moselle, a glass of dry champagne, two glasses of port, and a glass of dry brandy! He had taken laudanum the night before, again before breakfast, again last night, and again this morning.

It can't have come as much of a surprise, to Wellington at least, when the monarch passed away ten weeks later.

Somerset Maugham paid a visit to a peer whose notorious evening excesses detained him in bed long after most other people had risen and gone about their daily business. On inquiring at what hour his lordship breakfasted, Maugham was told by the butler, 'His Lordship does not breakfast, sir. His Lordship is usually sick at about eleven.'

The seventeenth century was a century for elaborate pies in England. One gets an idea of the sort of exotic creations that used to appear on well-to-do tables from the nursery rhyme:

> Sing a song of sixpence,
> A pocketful of rye,
> Four and twenty blackbirds
> Baked in a pie.
> When the pie was opened,
> The birds began to sing.
> Oh! wasn't that a dainty dish
> To set before a king.

The diocesan kitchens in Durham once turned out a pie that would have won a place in the *Guinness Book of Records*; it contained no less than 100 turkeys.

Dwarfs were sometimes hidden inside voluminous folds of pastry to jump out at a given moment for the amusement of their masters and their guests. And the celebrated English chef Robert

May described in his book, *The Accomplisht Cook*, which first appeared in 1660 (significantly, the year in which Charles II was restored to the throne), an enormous creation that consisted of 'The likeness of a ship of war in pasteboard', which was drawn into the dining-room on a cart to confront a castle fashioned from pasteboard and pastry. The castle was adorned with battlements, a portcullis and cannon charged with real gunpowder. In between stood a huge pastry stag filled with wine, flanked by two enormous pies (one filled with live blackbirds, the other with live frogs).

The fun started when one of the ladies present pulled an arrow from the stag. Out gushed its 'blood'. The cannon roared into action and the ladies threw eggshells of sweet water at each other in order to 'sweeten the stink of powder'. As this excitement was dying down, the lid of the frog pie was raised and 'out skip some frogs, which make the ladies to skip and shreek'. The blackbirds followed, blowing out the candles with their wings 'so that what with the flying birds and skipping frogs, the one above, the other beneath, will cause much delight and pleasure to the whole company'.

Apart from a chance drop of wine or a piece of passing pastry shrapnel, Master May's creation did not appear to offer the diner any sustenance. But then, one has heard similar complaints about the more excessive practitioners of *nouvelle cuisine*.

The court of Catherine the Great of Russia owed no obeisance to those in Paris or London. Extravagance and opulence knew no bounds there. The Empress maintained her own hothouses in which fresh vegetables and fruit were grown at unimaginable expense through the long Russian winter. Guests at one March dinner in St Petersburg were greeted by the sight of a real cherry tree laden with fruit. As an alternative (and a rather tastier one, by all accounts) fruit was regularly transported overland to the frozen capital from the warm coast of the Caspian Sea, a good 1,000 miles to the south.

The Russian court didn't stint itself either when it came to garnishing dishes. The British ambassador who was invited to the banquet celebrating the birth of the Empress's grandchild reported that, 'the dessert at supper was set out with jewels to the amount of upwards of two million sterling'.

It makes one wonder why the Russian Revolution was so long in coming.

The Prince Regent's chef Carême could never have been accused of misplaced modesty. Not above damning his fellow chefs for their 'miserable works which degrade our national cooking', adding 'Why are you so small in talent and so mean in invention?', he then laid down his criteria for the ideal cook, who should possess, 'a discerning and sensitive palate, perfect and exquisite taste, a strong and industrious character; he should be skilful and hardworking and unite delicacy, orde and economy'.

If these strictures seem a little extreme, one should remember that Carème practised ruthless self-control and self-denial in his own work. It wasn't unusual for work on the sauces of an important dinner to start at three in the morning, so that, by the time the first course was ready to be served, Carème had been on his feet for all day and half the night.

If that wasn't tiring enough, the kitchens of his day imposed their own demands. As he once wrote:

Imagine yourself in a large kitchen at the moment of a great dinner. See twenty chefs coming, going, moving with speed in this cauldron of heat, look at the mass of charcoal, a cubic metre for the cooking of entrées, and another mass on the ovens for the cooking of soups, sauces, ragouts, for frying and the water baths. Add to that a heap of burning wood in front of which four spits are turning, one of which bears a sirloin weighing forty-five to fifty pounds, the other fowl or game. In this furnace everyone moves with speed; not a sound is heard, only the chef has the right to speak and at the sound of his voice, everyone obeys. Finally the last straw: for about half an hour, all windows are closed so that the air does not cool the dishes as they are being served, and in this way we spend the best years of our lives. We must obey even when physical strength fails, but it is the burning charcoal that kills us.

In the early years of the last century, when much was said and heard about the epicurean indulgence of the Prince Regent, stimulated in no small measure by the masterly creations of Carême and others, there was a small but no less worthy movement dedicated to the same noble end of improving the nation's gastronomic awareness. This was the Eta Beta Pi, a dining club founded by William Kitchiner, an enthusiastic inventor and 'visionary'. (It was Kitchiner who advocated travelling on a cow for the simple reason that is assured a constant supply of fresh milk.)

The Eta Beta Pi was an institution that adhered to a strict code of practice. Kitchiner, who acted as secretary, was a stickler for punctuality. Latecomers were never allowed to take their seats at the table, in accordance with the dictum, 'the Secretary having represented that the perfections of several of the preparations is so exquisitely evanescent that the delay of one minute after their arrival at the meridian of concoction will render them no longer worthy of men of taste'.

Accordingly, those invited paid careful attention whenever invitations such as this arrived:

Dear Sir,

The honour of your company is requested to dine with the Committee of Taste, on Wednesday next, the 10th instant.

The specimens will be placed upon the table at five o'clock precisely, when the business of the day will immediately commence. I have the honour to be your most obedient servant.

William Kitchiner, Secretary
Eta Beta Pi

As an aid to furthering his own gastronomic sensibilities, Kitchiner developed his unique 'portable magazine of taste' - a boon to epicures like himself, who could not expect those with whom they were invited to dine to provide every essential condiment in addition to equipment indispensable to a man of taste.

The 'magazine' was kitted out with approaching thirty bottles of rudimentary items, like Kitchiner's own Wow-Wow sauce (a subtle blend of port, pickled cucumbers, capers and mustard). Other jars contained condiments like lemon peel, pickled walnuts, essence of celery and curaçao. Also included were handy items of tableware like a nutmeg grater, a pestle and mortar and a set of weights and measures.

In the days before every household provision was conveniently and appetizingly displayed on a supermarket shelf, a good part of the year in many households was spent bottling and preserving garden produce, in between attending to other domestic duties. In her *Book of Household Management*, Mrs Beeton offered her reader a breathless résumé of what might be expected in both quarters:

In June and July gooseberries, currants, raspberries, strawberries and other summer fruits should be preserved, and jams and jellies made. In July, too, the making of walnut ketchup should be attended to, as the green walnuts will be approaching perfection for this purpose. Mixed pickles may also now be made, and it will be found a good plan to have ready a jar of pickle-juice into which to put occasionally some young french beans or cauliflowers.

In the early autumn plums of various kinds are to be bottled and preserved and jams and jellies made. A little later, tomato sauce, a most useful article to have by you, may be prepared; a supply of apples laid in, if you have a place to keep them, as also a few keeping pears and filberts. Endeavour to keep also a large vegetable marrow – it will be found delicious in the winter.

In October and November it will be necessary to prepare for the cold weather, and get ready the winter clothing for the various members of the family. The white summer curtains will now be carefully put away, the fireplaces, grates and chimneys looked to, and the house put in a thorough state of repair, so that no 'loose tile' may, at a future day, interfere with your comfort, and extract something considerable from your pocket.

In December, the principal duty lies in preparing the creature comforts of those near and dear to us, so as to meet old Christmas with a happy face, a contented mind and a full larder; and in stoning the plums, washing the currants, cutting the citron, beating the eggs and mixing the pudding, a housewife is not unworthily greeting the genial season of all good things.

Happy she may well have been to reflect that Christmas comes but once a year!

If Mrs Beeton really did try all the recipes in her *Household Management*, the Beetons must have been treated to some pretty splendid eating, judging by the standards of most household fare these days. Even in the mid–1920s her style seemed a trifle overblown, as Wyndham Lewis implied in a parody he wrote in 1924:

MRS BEETON: This is a simple little sauce composed expressly for persons with limited incomes, and may be recommended to any housewife with frugal tastes and, indeed, to the poorest.

LORD HYBROUGH: Perhaps Mrs Beeton will reveal the secret? We (*He sweeps the whole room with a wide gesture*) we are all comrades here.

MRS BEETON (*coyly*): It is a very poor, unpretentious little thing. (*Closing her eyes.*) Take half a gallon of Napoleon brandy, place it in a sliver pan, rinse round and throw away. Next take five pounds of cream and break into it the yolks of thirty eggs. Whisk over a slow fire and set it on ice. Next take a quart of Imperial Tokay, three pounds of fine sugar, and ten lemons. Mix thoroughly, strain through the cream mixture and throw away. Take a dozen more eggs, beat lightly into a froth with two parts of good Madeira, squeeze the juice of a pound of hothouse grapes, and pour over the residue. After standing for an hour, strain the whole through a fine sieve and throw away as before. Repeat from the beginning, adding a magnum of champagne, the whites of two dozen plovers' eggs . . .

❋

Mrs Beeton's presence has cast such a shadow over the Victorian kitchen that many of her contemporary writers on home economics have been eclipsed. However, fifteen years before *Household Management* appeared, Alexis Soyer, writing in the enticingly named *Gastronomic Regenerator*, offered these tips under the uncompromising heading, 'How Everything Should Be in Cooking':

All clear soup must not be too strong of meat, and must be of a light brown, sherry, or straw colour.

All white or brown thick soups must be rather thinnish, lightly adhering to the back of the spoon.

All purées must adhere a little more to the back of the spoon.

Any Italian paste must be very clear, rather strong, and the colour of pale sherry.

All kinds of fish sauce should be thicker for boiled fish than for broiled or fried.

Brown sauce should be a little thinnish and the colour of a horse-chestnut.

Pheasants and partridges must be well done through, yet full of gravy.

Grouse, black cocks, gray hens, and ptarmigans

must cut reddish, with plenty of gravy, but not too much underdone.

All kinds of water-fowl must be very much underdone, so that the blood and gravy follow the knife in carving.

Plovers must be rather underdone, but done through.

Rabbits and pigeons must be well done.

Second-course savoury dishes must be rather highly seasoned, but with a little moderation.

Pastry should, when baked, be clear, light, and transparent, and of a beautiful straw colour; the body of a croustade the same.

Large pies, timbales, and casseroles of rice must be of a yellowish brown colour.

Jellies require to be very white and transparent for fruits, and not too firm, but better so than too delicate.

White sauce should be of the colour of ivory, and thicker than brown sauce.

Cream, or Dutch sauce, must be rather thickish, and cannot be too white.

Demi-glace requires to be thin, but sufficiently reduced to envelop pieces of meat, game, poultry, &c, with which it is served.

Every description of fish should be well done, but not over-boiled, broiled, stewed, or fried.

Beef and mutton must be underdone even for joints, removes, and entrées.

Lamb requires to be more done.

Veal and pork must be well done.

Venison must be underdone, red in the middle, and full of gravy, but not raw.

Poultry, either broiled, stewed, boiled, or roasted, must be done throughly, not cutting in the least red, but must still be full of gravy.

Orange jellies should be of a deep orange colour, and all fruit jellies as near as possible to the colour of the fruit.

Creams should be very light and delicate, but fruit creams must be kept of the colour of the fruits they are made of.

For all the demi-glace removes the ice must be firm, but not in the least hard.

All kinds of soufflé or fondu must be well done through, or they would be very indigestible, clog the delicate palate, and prevent the degustation of the generous claret which flows so freely after dinner on the table of the real epicure.

I recommend sugar in almost all savoury dishes, as it greatly facilitates digestion and invigorates the palate, but always increase or diminish the quantity according to the taste of your employer.

I often introduce onions, eschalots, or even a little garlic in some of my most delicate dishes, but so well blended that I never have a single objection even by those who have a great dislike to it.

Horseradish and herbs of every description may always be used with discretion to great advantage.

Contrary to the expressed opinion of every other previous publication, I say that too much seasoning is preferable to too little, as your employer can correct you by saying there is too much of this or that, and you can soon get it to his taste; but while you fear over-seasoning you produce no flavour at all; by allowing each guest to season for himself, your sauce attains a diversity of flavours. The cook must season for the guest, not the guest for the cook.

I have always found great advantage in dressing the greatest part of my entrées on a thin roll of mashed potatoes; this has never been found objectionable, as it is so thin that it is imperceptible when covered with the sauces, and serves to prevent any entrées when dressed in crown from being upset, before going on table, by the carelessness of the servant.

My mother was a kind of totally fiendish, al fresco eater and throughout my childhood I was subjected to picnics throughout the twelve months of the year. We had relations who lived in Nottinghamshire and it used to be arranged that we would meet half-way between them and our home in Liverpool. A cursory glance at the map will show that our rendezvous was invariably right up in the Pennines. There we would gather in February, high on the bleak moors, to shelter in the lee of the cars drinking tins of soup and piping hot coffee for the apparent good of our health; as far as my mother was concerned, picnics and the seasons knew no parting of the ways. It took me many years to eat a salad with any degree of enjoyment.

Mrs Beeton offers no tips on the weather for her picnics but judging by the staggering amount of food (not to mention the quantities of 'beverages' and their accompanying '3 corkscrews') that she lists, my dear mother would have approved wholeheartedly. This is what Mrs Beeton suggested as a 'Bill of fare for a picnic for 40 persons':

A joint of cold roast beef, a joint of cold boiled beef, 2 ribs of lamb, 2 shoulders of lamb, 4 roast fowls, 2 roast ducks, 1 ham, 1 tongue, 2 veal-and-ham pies, 2 pigeon pies, 6 medium-sized lobsters, 1 piece of collared calf's head, 18 lettuces, 6 baskets of salad, 6 cucumbers.

Stewed fruit well sweetened, and put into glass bottles well corked; 3 or 4 dozen plain pastry biscuits to eat with the stewed fruit, 2 dozen fruit turnovers, 4 dozen cheesecakes, 2 cold cabinet puddings in moulds, 2 blancmanges in moulds, a few jam puffs, 1 large cold plum-pudding (this must be good), a few baskets of fresh fruit, 3 dozen plain biscuits, a piece of cheese, 6 lbs of butter (this, of course, includes the butter for tea), 4 quartern loaves of household bread, 3 dozen rolls, 6 loaves of tin bread (for tea), 2 plain plum cakes, 2 pound cakes, 2 sponge cakes, a tin of mixed biscuits, ½ lb of tea. Coffee is not suitable for a picnic, being difficult to make.

Under 'Things not be forgotten at a Picnic' the inestimable lady lists:

A stick of horseradish, a bottle of mint-sauce well corked, a bottle of salad dressing, a bottle of vinegar, made mustard, pepper, salt, good oil, and pounded sugar. If it can be managed, take a little ice. It is scarcely necessary to say that plates, tumblers, wine-glasses, knives, forks, and spoons, must not be forgotten; as also teacups and saucers, 3 or 4 teapots, some lump sugar, and milk, if this last-named article cannot be obtained in the neighbourhood. Take 3 corkscrews.

Beverages. – 3 dozen quart bottles of ale, packed in hampers; ginger-beer, soda-water, and lemonade, of each 2 dozen bottles; 6 bottles of sherry, 6 bottles of claret, champagne a discretion, and any other light wine that may be preferred, and 2 bottles of brandy. Water can usually be obtained so it is useless to take it.

The spirit of balance and harmony that characterized the artistic flowering of the Renaissance found its own outlet in the kitchen. The French essayist Montaigne described the new order when he wrote of his meeting with the master cook of the Neapolitan Cardinal Caraffa, who was ultimately banished from Rome for extortion. Of his cook Montaigne wrote:

> With magisterial gravity, he delivered me a discourse on this science of food – first about the general composition of the sauces, and then describing in detail the nature of their ingredients and their effects; then about the differences in salads according to the season: what should be heated and what should be served cold, and the way to garnish and embellish them to please the eye. After that he came to describing the order of service, full of fine and important considerations; the whole overlaid with rich and high-sounding words that are generally used to report upon the government of an empire.

400 years later Seymour Britchky, the New York restaurant critic, was saying something very similar about the waiters in one Manhattan restaurant, who apparently discussed the menu with you, 'as if they were sharing wisdom picked up in the Himalayas'.

The study of the eating habits of the lion convinced Dr George Fordyce, one of London's leading medical authorities at the end of the eighteenth century, that one meal a day was all that *Homo sapiens* required as well. In pursuit of this principle, he followed the same pattern of dining for twenty years, taking himself every afternoon at four o'clock to Dolly's Chop House in Paternoster Row, where he tucked into half a chicken or a plate of boned fish while awaiting the arrival of his daily one and a half pounds of rump steak. To wash this down he used to take a tankard of strong ale, a bottle of port and a quarter pint of brandy. From Dolly's he then progressed to three coffee houses, in each of which he downed a brandy and water. It wasn't until he was past his sixty-second year that gout finally got the better of him and carried him off.

To celebrate the return of Philip Stanhope from the Grand Tour, his father, the Earl of Chesterfield (and author of the celebrated series of letters on the correct deportment of the eighteenth-century gentleman), held a magnificent banquet at Chesterfield House, no doubt hoping that young Philip would display some of the polish and savoir-faire that his father earnestly hoped had rubbed off on him during his time on the Continent. His hopes were sadly dashed by 'an oval dish containing a quantity of excellent baked gooseberries, then a rarity, snowed under with a rich covering of whipped cream'. With mounting horror and chagrin, Lord Chesterfield watched Philip assault this with spectacular greed.

His first helping was gross enough, but having finished that off, he called back the servant who was carrying away the dish, took it from him, held it under his chin and 'lapped it in hasty spoonfuls', liberally spraying his cheeks with lashings of cream.

'John, why don't you fetch a strop and razor?' said the earl to his son's valet, vainly trying to gloss over the incident. 'You can see your master is going to shave himself.'

A national bread strike a few years ago had a special impact on customers who bought their provisions at one of the principal grocers in Mayfair. Anyone asking for bread received the reply that every loaf and roll in the shop had been bought early in the morning by an Arab who had also purchased its entire stock of yeast as well as 36 lb of flour.

Anthony Trollope never experienced difficulties where food was concerned. To a lady who noticed that he helped himself generously from every dish offered to him and who volunteered the remark, 'You seem to have a very good appetite, Mr Trollope', the novelist replied, 'None at all, madam. But thank God I am very greedy.'

In the course of gathering material for his book *A Ramble Through Normandy*, published in 1855, George M Musgrave was fascinated by the sight of a midday meal consumed by a couple he took to be on their honeymoon. The setting was a river steamer on the Seine at Rouen. The happy pair seated themselves, surveyed the menu and kicked off with soup. Fried mackerel, steak served with French beans and fried potatoes followed. Then came an *omelette aux fines herbes*, a *fricandeau* of veal with sorrel, a roast chicken with mushrooms and a hock of ham with spinach. An apricot tart came next, pursued by three custards and a salad that heralded a small roast leg of lamb garnished with chopped onion and nutmeg. Coffee, two glasses of absinthe, and *eau dorée* provided a slight pause in the repast before they set to again with cheese, fruit and cakes. Two hours were needed to see the pair through their lunch, during which Musgrave noted that they were sustained by two bottles of Burgundy and one of Chablis.

Harold Nicolson used to tell of a gourmet of his acquaintance who was both 'inordinately greedy and inordinately rich'. Every day he delighted in preparing a favourite soup for his guests. Into a silver cauldron he tipped exotic olives, a lobster, bottles of Veuve Clicquot and amontillado sherry. Harold Nicolson's assessment was that this bizarre brew tasted like 'very hot cough mixture drunk with shrimp sauce'.

Artistic praise comes in many forms though few divas can have received the plaudit awarded to Adelina Patti by Rossini, who congratulated her with the words, 'Madame, I have cried only twice in my life, once when I dropped a wing of truffled chicken into Lake Como, and once when for the first time I heard you sing.'

❋

George Frederick Handel was an accomplished trencherman. The story is told of the time he ordered dinner for two at a local tavern. When the food was brought to him the landlord saw only Handel and commented that he had been led to understand that the great composer was expecting company.

'I am the company,' Handel told him, settling down to work his way through both dinners.

Brahms was also very partial to his food and was less than thrilled when he became ill and was instructed to go on a diet. 'But this evening I am dining with Strauss,' he protested to his doctor, 'and we shall have chicken paprika.'

'That's quite out of the question,' the doctor told him.

'In that case,' said Brahms, 'please consider that I did not come to consult you until tomorrow.'

Conversation Piece

Arranging guests at a dinner party is a definite art. There are some who are superb raconteurs without actually being frightfully good conversationalists. Surround them with people who are happy to be entertained, however, wind them up and let them go, and you can enjoy a splendid evening.

Then there are those who can stimulate each other like a chemical reaction, producing conversation that is truly wondrous.

And there are guests, like Robert Morley, who are a law unto themselves. It always seems so unlikely, when you hear Robert expounding his deeply left-wing views, that it can be a slightly unsettling experience for those who don't know him. As what must have sounded like an active member of the Workers' Revolutionary Party, he deeply shocked a couple of Australian dowagers with whom we invited him to dinner one night with his ultra-communistic conversation.

After the good ladies had departed, I asked whether I could drop him anywhere.

'Oh, yes, dear,' he replied. 'Perhaps you'd like to drop me off at the Ritz, dear. I'm going to play the tables in Monte Carlo, dear, and I always like staying at the Ritz because it's so delightfully shabby.'

So off I drove my left-wing revolutionary friend to the Ritz.

Clement Freud can be mildly unnerving, too, as a guest. The first time he ever came to dinner my poor wife was absolutely terrified. She cooked a most elaborate meal, at the end of which Clement commented, 'I must say, I think the bread's very nice.'

131

The Victorians knew all about the art of table talk. At least the author of *Conversational Openings: Some Hints for the Game of Small Talk* presumably thought he did when offering these telling words of advice. (His contribution formed part of a wider series that came under the compelling general heading *The Dullard's Handbook Series*.)

'All I wish to do is to suggest a few formulas which may prove useful to the dull,' he modestly informs his readers by way of introduction; 'a series of Conversational Openings, so to speak, in the sense of Chess openings, the acquirement of which will lead insensibly to mastering the next step.'

In pursuit of his 'dream . . . to hide the joins of life, as it were, to fill up some of the unsightly gaps of existence', he propounds the worthy maxim, 'One platitude at the right moment is worth a dozen repartees the next morning.'

Getting down to business, the author offers the reader a number of everyday situations, plucked from life's maelstrom with the same cheerful confidence as those presented in foreign language phrase books. This is what he has to say:

At Table

If the players are unequally matched:

Black (Man)
(1) Do you say drink soup, or eat soup?

White (Lady)
(1) I really don't know – I don't think I say either.

| (2) What do you say, then? | (2) I really don't know – I don't think I say anything. |

If the players are well matched:

Black (Man)	White (Lady)
(1) Do you say eat soup, or drink soup?	(1) That is a question I have spent my life trying to solve.
(2) You may not say 'take' it either, I believe.	(2) No, certainly not! It is a most difficult problem, etc.

This is a promising beginning, and should within six or seven remarks lead to a discussion on the influence of contemporary fashion on the transformation of the language.

Temperance Opening

| Black (Man) | White (Lady) |
| (1) Might I ask you to pass me the water? | (1) Certainly. Are you a teetotaller? |

In four moves Man should now be in the middle of the discussion on temperance.

Geographical Opening

This will succeed where almost every other fails

and besides, it can be combined with the well-worn Weather Opening, eg:

Black (Man)
(1) How wretched the weather has been!

(2) Really! Are you a cockney?

White (Lady)
(1) Yes, indeed, though I ought to be accustomed to the weather in London, as it is my native air.

Aunt's Friend's Opening

White (Lady)
(1) I think you know my aunt.
(2) Yes, Mrs Mackay.

Black (Man)
(1) Your aunt?

(2) Oh, to be sure, yes – we met in the Engadine last year.

This can always be combined with the Geographical Opening.

After Dinner Opening

Black (Man)
(1) We have been having a most interesting discussion since you left us.

White (Lady)
(1) Indeed. What about?

This, of course, assumes that Black has some

foundation for his assertion. It would not do to begin thus:

Black (Man)
(1) I have eaten a whole dish of almonds and raisins since we parted.

Lord Curzon dined early one evening at White's and, finding only one other member seated at the long table, felt obliged to exchange a few general remarks with him. His fellow diner replied by inquiring how Curzon proposed to spend the rest of the evening.

Curzon said he would be going to see a play, *Diplomacy*, for the second time; something he rarely did. His companion said he would be going as well – for the eighty-seventh time. Curzon was amazed and expressed the opinion that neither the cast nor the play deserved such a compliment. Their conversation rather petered out after that. But before they parted the other diner remarked, 'By the way, my name is Coghlan.'

He was the actor playing the lead in Curzon's entertainment that evening.

Somerset Maugham put forward the suggestion that, 'At a dinner party one should talk wisely but not too well, and talk well but not too wisely.'

According to A A Milne, 'It is only the very young girl at her first dinner party whom it is difficult to entertain. At her second dinner party, and thereafter, she knows the whole art of being amusing. All she has to do is listen; all we men have to do is to tell her about ourselves.'

J M Barrie was in this very predicament on one occasion, seated beside a girl who was as easy on the eye as she seemed empty-headed. After a slightly awkward lull in their conversation the girl asked, 'Not all your plays are a success, I suppose, Sir James?'

'No, my dear,' he replied. 'Some Peter out and some Pan out.'

Barrie used to enjoy pulling Bernard Shaw's leg about his vegetarianism. The two of them were invited to lunch on one occasion and, while the rest of the company were presented with what Barrie considered to be more palatable fare, Shaw was offered a selection of salads, dressed with a range of mayonnaises and oils. Watching Shaw as he raised the first forkful to his mouth, Barrie inquired, 'Tell me, Shaw, have you eaten that, or are you just about to?'

At a literary lunch held in honour of Arnold Bennett, the author was asked to sign copies of his latest book. Among his fans was a young man who arrived carrying three copies. Too embarrassed to ask Bennett to sign all three at once, he presented the first, had that autographed and then returned to the back of the queue, in the hope that Bennett wouldn't recognize him when he presented volume number two. The second book was signed without any apparent recognition and the young man returned to the back of the queue once more. When he handed Bennett his third copy, there was a brief pause before he wrote the young man's name, adding, 'who is fast becoming an old friend'.

During the course of a dinner in which Lord and Lady Birkenhead were the guests of honour, one of the other guests asked Lord Birkenhead (F E Smith) what he considered the three great milestones in his life.

After a few moments reflection, F E replied, 'The first when I heard that I'd got a double first at Oxford. I suppose the second was when I was made a KC, and the third was when I became Lord Chancellor.'

His wife then chipped in by asking, 'But darling, what about the day we got married?'

'My dear,' replied her husband without hesitation, 'I think you must be getting a little deaf. We are talking about milestones – not millstones.'

There is, I am told, a wealthy patroness of the arts resident in the smartest area of Philadelphia who down the years has shown a remarkable degree of hospitality to visiting actors appearing in the city's Walnut Street Theatre.

In addition to the generosity she shows in providing both bed and board, she has a conversational quality that doesn't so much lubricate the talk around her table as give it a hefty shot of high-octane additive. At one celebrated dinner a more diffident member of the company who repeatedly refused a second helping was given the final encouragement by his hostess, 'Come along, you can eat it now and vomit later.'

A non-smoker herself, she at least makes a minor concession to those who do indulge in the pleasures of tobacco, proffering a handsome silver cigarette case with the airy entreaty, 'Cancer, anyone?'

Not long after her marriage to the last white rajah of Sarawak, Sylvia Brooke held a dinner party. To begin with the conversation was a bit sticky and at one stage silence reigned for an agonizingly long period. Then a welcome sound wafted into the room, allowing Sylvia Brooke to say gaily, 'How wonderful. It's started to rain at last.'

All eyes turned to the open window and the veranda beyond, where the old rajah was standing contentedly spending a penny on the shrubbery below.

The dramatist Douglas Jerrold found himself trapped next to an insufferable bore at dinner and sat mutely through several courses while his neighbour displayed his intellectual prowess. Warming to his subject, this fellow went as far as to compare himself to the great medieval scholar Peter Abelard and his wife to Abélard's celebrated mistress, Héloïse. His good lady had been raised in a convent, he went on to explain, and had been on the point of taking the veil when they met.

Seemingly, his manifold gifts had won her heart, leading her to renounce her calling and accept his offer of marriage.

'Ah,' replied Jerrold, 'she evidently thought you better than nun.'

A similarly self-satisfied young bore dominated the conversation when he sat next to Bernard Shaw at a dinner party, talking interminably and revealing himself to be a repository of useless information.

'You know, between the two of us we know all there is to know,' Shaw told him as they were leaving the table.

'How is that?' he was asked.

'Well,' said Shaw, 'you seem to know every-thing, except that you are a bore. And I know that.'

A hostess sitting at the opposite end of the table to a great friend scribbled a note to her during a dinner party and asked the butler to deliver it discreetly. Unfortunately, the lady couldn't read without her glasses. So she asked the man seated on her left to help her out.

'Please be a dear,' he read, 'and try to liven up the man on your left. He's a terrible bore, but see if you can talk to him.'

The story is told of a lunch party given in the British Embassy in Cairo shortly after the ambassador, Sir Miles Lampson, had become Lord Killearn. Among those present was a lady who confided to the ambassador's wife, 'It's so nice that you're here now and not those Lampsons, whom everybody disliked so much.'

The moment that the guests were seated at an embassy dinner, one of the ladies present started to complain that, according to precedence, she should have been sitting next to the ambassador, and not several places down the table, as was the case. A couple of discreet inquiries confirmed that she was actually right and the whole line of guests rose and rearranged themselves to make room for her. Seated triumphantly in her rightful seat, she apologized to her host for any confusion she had caused, saying, 'I expect you and your wife find these questions of protocol extremely troublesome, your Excellency.'

'Not really,' replied the ambassador. 'Experience has taught that those who matter don't mind and those who mind don't matter.'

After a photographic session with Yousef Karsh, the astronaut Neil Armstrong was invited to stay to lunch with the photographer and his wife. For much of the time Armstrong asked questions about the many different countries that the couple had visited in the course of their work.

'But Mr Armstrong,' said Mrs Karsh at one point, 'you have walked on the moon. We want to hear about your travels.'

'But that's the only place I've ever been,' he said apologetically.

During the war the Astors held a house party at Cliveden and included the Labour politician and trade unionist Jimmy Thomas among their guests. When he arrived Nancy Astor asked Thomas what he might talk about if she invited him to say a few words to the rest of the party.

'How about my telling them what the Labour Party is going to do with this house, if it gets into power after the war?' he replied.

'My own suggestion,' answered his hostess, 'is that you turn it into a boarding house and make me the landlady. Though in that case, Mr Thomas, you'd have to pay for your board and lodging, which you have never done in the past.'

An anti-Semitic nobleman seated next to Sir Moses Montefiore opened their conversation with the playful gambit, 'I have just returned from Japan, and it's a most unusual country. Did you know that it has neither pigs nor Jews?'

'In that case,' replied Sir Moses, 'we should go there together, so the Japanese will have a sample of each.'

The writer Oliver Herford was enjoying a quiet lunch one day when a man for whom he had a particular loathing approached him and slapped him heartily on the back with a cheery grin and a jovial, 'How are you doing, Ollie, old boy?'

'I don't know your name,' said Herford coldly. 'I don't know your face. But your manners are very familiar.'

The French novelist and playwright Tristan Bernard had a particular antipathy towards women journalists. He certainly didn't warm to the one he was next to at a press lunch who said as they took their seats, 'Forget that I am a woman. Treat me as you would a male colleague.'

Throughout the meal Bernard totally ignored her. Only when lunch was finished did he turn to her and say, 'Allons pisser.'

As a young man, the Victorian diplomat and politician Henry Labouchère was dining in his club one evening and took the opportunity to indulge in a good many racy stories with his friends. Their conversation was not to the liking of one of the elder members of the club, who pushed aside his unfinished meal, rose from the table and told Labouchère sternly, 'Do you realize, sir, that I knew your grandmother?'

'I had no idea, sir,' said Labouchère, also rising to his feet, before adding politely, 'Do I, perhaps, have the honour of addressing my grandfather?'

As might be expected from the architect of the German Empire, Prince Otto von Bismarck was a stickler for formality. A young American woman seated next to him at lunch one day addressed her opening remarks to him correctly with the title 'Your Highness'. By the time the second course appeared this had become 'Mr Chancellor'. A course later and she was calling him 'My dear Mr Bismarck'. As the waiters removed their plates Bismarck smiled and said, 'My first name is Otto.'

The restaurateur Victor Sassie tells the story of a dinner party he was asked to arrange in honour of the Chinese ambassador. The host for the evening explained that His Excellency seldom dined outside the embassy and, when he did, never ate a morsel.

However, when the first course of wild cherry soup was served, the ambassador was invited to taste it and, contrary to expectations, consumed it all approvingly. In fact, the whole meal turned out to be a gastronomic *tour de force*.

As he was making ready to leave, the ambassador thanked Victor Sassie through an interpreter, explaining that in the course of his official duties he attended many functions and had to watch his weight. However, he'd found Victor's meal irresistible.

Understandably delighted by this, Victor replied that he was most grateful and was 'happy to have found a chink in the armour'.

'I have made a bet, Mr Coolidge,' said a young guest seated next to America's thirtieth and most taciturn president, 'that I could get more than two words out of you.'

'You lose,' replied her host, honouring his nickname – 'Silent Cal'.

Lord Castlerosse was a Falstaffian figure of the old school – a huge, all-consuming clown of a man with a quick wit hidden inside his massive frame. Playing golf with Nancy Cunard one day, she asked him what his handicap was.

'Drink and debauchery,' he answered her – rueful but right.

Following this theme, Castlerosse was out to dinner one evening when the lady beside him, who knew him of old, poked him playfully in the bulging midriff and said, 'Rossie, this is a disgrace. If I saw it on a girl I'd say she was pregnant!'

'Madam,' Castlerosse replied, 'it has been and she is.'

Lord Haldane, sometime Lord Chancellor and Secretary for War in the early years of this century, was built along similarly corpulent lines. However, he staunchly maintained that a surplus of flesh did not necessarily indicate a deficit of fitness. He proved the point one evening after dinner in London when he had received some gentle ribbing about his size. Rising from his seat, he announced that he would set off to walk to Brighton then and there in his evening clothes, allowing himself no more than two minutes' rest in every hour and sending a telegram to his fellow diners when he arrived at his destination, sixty miles away. With that he left the room and did exactly as he had pledged. ✳

In 1867 Karl Marx published the first volume of *Das Kapital*, Henrik Ibsen published *Peer Gynt* and the world of social intercourse was made the richer by the publication of *How to Shine in Society: or the Art of Conversation*. Among the gems of advice it offers the reader are these:

In general people who have not been introduced are not understood to be on conversing terms. In travelling more freedom is allowed, but even then the conversation is but very general unless special circumstances warrant otherwise.

Who should begin a conversation is not easy to say. Where there is doubt as to who should begin, let it be the person of the greatest importance in the company. But if it be done modestly any one may begin.

But it is not so difficult to begin a conversation as it is to carry it on successfully. Wit is by no means a sure card. Few can play it well, and still fewer maintain the play. Nor will learning supply you with the material of the right sort altogether. That must pass through the alembic of your mind and give forth its fine precipitate of thought, and this brings us to the stuff of the proper kind for conversation purposes, for conversation is but the interchange of thought. Learning is dead inert matter that begets nothing. It is thought that makes words winged, and hours too.

Look the person in the face with whom you are conversing. Never talk past him – it gives you an air of insincerity. Let your manner be confident without being bold, and easy without being familiar.

Talk neither too slowly nor too quickly, but with a lively degree of raciness. Animation is indispensable to successful conversation. Let the tones of your voice be as musical as possible, steering equally clear of 'clipping' the words of their due amount of sound, or of mouthing them with too much.

In general society never allude to private matters. Talk with the company on subjects of general interest. With learned men you may talk of learned subjects, but never inflict your superior knowledge on people of lesser pretensions. It would be like a rich man displaying his gold against a poorer man's copper. Never interrupt a speaker in what he is saying. If you step before him unceremoniously, it is courteous of him indeed, if he does not take the tempting opportunity of using his foot to take you out of the way.

Never crush any subject of conversation and substitute one of your own in its stead. If you wish it changed, wait till it is exhausted, or lead it in the direction of your own.

Never converse with a pre-occupied mind. Throw your whole mind into it, else you are sure to make the conversation hard and drag 'its weary weight along'.

If unable or not disposed to talk on a subject, you can listen.

The 4th Earl of Chesterfield laboured long and hard, and with little visible sign of success, in moulding his natural son, Philip Stanhope, into something approaching a gentleman. Countless letters of instruction flowed from his lordship's pen, as well as advice on every aspect of correct form.

Lord Chesterfield had a particular abhorrence of laughter, of which he wrote:

Having mentioned laughing, I must particularly warn you against it: and I could heartily wish that you may often be seen to smile, but never heard to laugh. Frequent and loud laughter is the characteristic of folly and ill manners: it is the manner in which the mob express their silly joy at silly things . . . in my mind there is nothing so illiberal, and so ill-bred, as audible laughter.

During his time as a young army officer Winston Churchill grew a moustache. This was picked on by a grand dowager with whom he was arguing at an equally grand dinner. In an attempt to silence the impudent young man the lady retorted, 'Mr Churchill, I care for neither your politics nor your moustache.'

'Madam,' Churchill answered, 'you are unlikely to come into contact with either.'

Mrs Patrick Campbell, who was not noted for her forbearance, was seated once at dinner beside a zoologist whose speciality was ants. He talked endlessly about the industry of these remarkable insects, the social organization of their colonies and their clearly defined pecking order. By way of emphasis, he told her enthusiastically, 'Do you know, they have their army and their own police force?'

'What, no navy?' replied Mrs Pat.

When Clement Attlee was prime minister he invited Sir John Gielgud to supper at Stratford after the theatre. Gielgud sat next to Attlee's daughter and they fell into conversation on where they lived.

'I have a very convenient home in Westminster,' said Sir John. 'So easy to walk to the theatre. And where do you live?'

'Number 10 Downing Street,' was the surprised and slightly frosty reply.

Before his election as Pope John XXIII, Angelo Roncalli was made the first papal nuncio to France after the end of the last war. Invited to a banquet in Paris, he was seated next to a lady wearing a dress with a provocatively cut neckline, which the future pope appeared not to notice. When fruit was served, however, he offered a large juicy apple to the lady, which she politely refused.

'Please take it, madam,' he said. 'It was only after Eve ate the apple that she became aware of how little she had on.'

Charlie Chaplin used to enjoy entertaining his guests with impressions of other celebrities. At the end of one dinner party, he sang an operatic aria with such style that one of his guests exclaimed that he never knew Chaplin could sing so beautifully.

'I can't sing at all,' replied his host. 'I was only imitating Caruso.'

On the subject of table talk, Mrs Beeton had this to say:

In conversation, trifling occurrences, such as small disappointments, petty annoyances and other everyday incidents should never be mentioned to your friends. The extreme injudiciousness of repeating these will be at once apparent when we reflect on the unsatisfactory discussions which they too frequently occasion, and on the load of advice which they are the cause of being tendered, and which is too often of a kind neither to be useful nor agreeable. Greater events, whether of joy or sorrow, should be communicated to friends; and, on such occasions, their sympathy gratifies and comforts. If the mistress be a wife, never let an account of her husband's failings pass her lips; and in cultivating the power of conversation, she should keep the versified advice of Cowper continually in her memory, that it:

Should flow like water after summer showers,
Nor as if raised by mere mechanic powers.

In reference to its style, Dr Johnson, who was himself greatly distinguished for his colloquial abilities, says that 'no style is more extensively acceptable than the narrative, because this does not carry an air of superiority over the rest of the company, and therefore is most likely to please them. For this purpose we should store our memory with short anecdotes and entertaining pieces of history. Almost everyone listens with eagerness to contemporary history.' Vanity often co-operates with curiosity, for he that is a hearer in one place wishes to qualify himself to be a principal speaker in some inferior company, and therefore more attention is given to narrations than anything else in conversation, but they frequently tend to raise envy in some of the company.

❋

A guest seated immediately to the left of the Queen watched her being served first with asparagus and realized that as the dish moved round the table he would be served last. This gave him ample time to observe how Her Majesty coped with the delicious, but notoriously messy, delicacy. However, when his turn came, the Queen said with a smile, 'Now it's my turn to see you make a pig of yourself.'

Her Majesty's grandfather, King George V, once sought to put a lady guest at ease, after her hat pin had fallen into her soup, by asking, 'Did you come here expecting to eat winkles?'

When C S Lewis was up for election as a fellow of Magdalen College, Oxford, he was invited to dine in hall to be scrutinized closely by the President and other members of the senior common room. The President of Magdalen in those days was the intimidating figure of Sir Herbert Warren and it was next to him that Lewis was seated at high table. Not a word passed between them for two courses, but with the arrival of the meat the President asked, 'Do you like poetry, Mr Lewis?'

'Yes, President, I do,' he answered. This elicited no response from Sir Herbert, so the young candidate added, 'I also like prose.'

That seemed to conclude their conversation, for nothing more passed between them, though Lewis was awarded his fellowship.

At the age of sixty-eight Richard Chevenix Trench, former Dean of Westminster and Archbishop of Dublin, suffered a serious fall which broke both his knees and from which he never really recovered. The story is told of the time he was sitting at dinner when the lady beside him heard mutterings to the effect, 'It's come at last. I can't feel a thing. I'm paralysed.'

Asking him what was the matter, she was told, 'I've been pinching my leg for the last five minutes and I can't feel a thing. I'm paralysed.'

With an unavoidable colour rising to her cheeks, his neighbour had to confess that it had been her leg to which he had been paying such careful and earnest attention.

The artist James Whistler seems an unlikely product of the US military academy at West Point and in a way he was, since he failed his exams there and was obliged to seek an alternative profession. At one point he went before a committee of examiners and appalled them by not knowing the date of the Battle of Buena Vista.

'Suppose you went out to dinner,' said one of the military man in horror, 'and the company got to talking about the Mexican War, and you, a West Point man, did not know the date of this battle. What would you do?'

'I should refuse to associate with people who

talked of such things at dinner,' Whistler answered firmly.

The couturier Norman Hartnell was lunching in the country one day when a lull in the conversation allowed him the opportunity to compliment his hostess on the splendid silver trophy that decorated the centre of the table.

Beaming with pride she told him, 'I won it for one of my jumpers.'

'How very clever of you,' he said. 'Could you knit one for me?'

Her enthusiasm for riding once led Princess Anne to spend an entire meal talking to the man sitting on one side of her, while completely ignoring the man on the other side. It wasn't until coffee was served that she spoke to him and then it was only to ask, 'Could I have the sugar, please?' In reply she was offered two lumps held out in the palm of his hand.

It is claimed, though I have no personal experience to confirm it, that one sure way a lady has of ridding herself of unwanted suitors is to invite them to dinner – but no ordinary dinner, by all accounts.

The menu runs something like: cream of mushroom soup, dover sole, chicken suprême and any soufflé you care to mention, as long as it is white.

To complement this the hostess must dress entirely in white as well, and to complete the ensemble the meal must be served on a plain linen table cloth, laid with plain white plates and ivory-handled cutlery.

Apparently the effect of this display of pristine purity is more then enough to cool the flames of passion in the most red-blooded admirer.

Unaccustomed As I Am

I ought to say at the outset that although I do quite a bit of after-dinner speaking, and won a Benedictine after-dinner speaker of the year award in 1989, which rather negates the 'unaccustomed bit', there are still occasions when the experience can be distinctly unnerving.

Not long ago I was invited to address a gathering of the British Tie-Makers' Association. When I arrived I was greeted with the sad news that an eminent member of this fraternity had died and that his party had withdrawn as an act of respect. Furthermore, each place they would have occupied was marked by a wreath. Getting up to deliver some vaguely witty words in this somewhat sombre presence didn't make for the easiest or most sparkling performance.

I've had my share of difficulties speaking overseas, too. I still blush at the memory of an invitation I had to speak in New Zealand at a Zontian lunch, a sort of ladies Rotarian get-together. Madam Chairman was a local headmistress and all through lunch I was worried by a hair that kept wafting in front of her mouth. I had an image of the poor darling swallowing this when she got up to introduce me, so when the moment came I reached over to remove the hair, with a deferential, 'Excuse me, headmistress.'

The hair turned out to be a whisker attached to a mole and in front of 300 women there was I pulling the headmistress towards me by this appendage.

I remember Clement Freud telling me how much he enjoyed it when he began after-dinner speaking. Indeed, meeting Bob Monkhouse one day, they began chatting about their respective experiences and Clement spoke warmly about the pleasure he got from being invited to speak to a wide variety of audiences. He asked Bob what he got out of it.

'Forty-five quid,' was the answer and food for some thought.

So the next time Clement was invited to say a few words he mentioned a fee of £45.

'£45?' asked his would-be host in some amazement.

'Yes, I'm afraid so,' answered Clement.

'But for £45 we could get Bob Monkhouse!' And that was that.

Perhaps a little jaundiced by this experience, Clement once gave Kenneth Williams some advice on public speaking after a session of recording *Just a Minute*. Kenneth had been asked to speak at a literary lunch and wanted to pick Clement's brain for a few tips.

'Criticize the menu,' was the advice. 'It works like a dream. They always give you the same things, so start with that. Tell them the menu is unadventurous: dreary prawn cocktail – why not use a little imagination? Half-a-dozen oysters would have been delightful.'

'Aren't they an aphrodisiac?' asked Kenneth.

'Yes,' said Clement. 'If you don't swallow them quickly, your neck goes stiff.'

We never did hear how Kenneth got on at that do.

The mention of literary lunches brings to mind the invitation I received to address one of these erudite gatherings arranged by *Age* newspaper in Australia. I had prepared what I considered a few suitably literary thoughts to get me started, but when it came to the event, these were somewhat at odds with the remarkable introduction I received.

The Australian gentleman speaking in advance of me to warm things up clearly enjoyed a racier literary fare than I had anticipated. He spoke in the most uproarious way and his last joke and closing words went rather like this:

This lady comes into a corner shop and says to the shopkeeper, 'I'd like a tin of Pedigree Chum, please.'

The next day she comes back for another tin, and the day after that and so on.

'What do you want all that for?' says the shopkeeper after several visits. 'You must have a lot of dogs?'

'No – it's for my husband. He won't eat anything else,' says the lady. 'He loves Pedigree Chum.'

'You can't give him Pedigree Chum,' says the shopkeeper. 'You can't give him that. It's not fit for human consumption. Can't you give him something else to eat? You know, it's absolutely fatal to a man to eat Pedigree Chum.'

'Well, he won't eat anything else at all. He just

loves Pedigree Chum.'

About four weeks later she comes in again, but this time she is dressed all in black. 'Can I have a lettuce and some carrots' she asks.

'Is that for your husband?' asks the shopkeeper.

'No, he's dead.'

'Well, I told you. I told you. You shouldn't have let him eat that Pedigree Chum.'

'Oh, it wasn't that,' she said. 'He was in the middle of the road licking his dick and he was run over by a lorry.'

Now I'd like to introduce Mr Derek Nimmo. Mr Derek Nimmo, I'd like to call upon you to address our literary gathering.

Having to follow that left me frankly speechless. My merry opening gambit, which ran along the lines of wondering whether or not I should accept the invitation and deciding there was nothing to be lost by it (after all, what would have happened if Michelangelo had said to Pope Julius II, 'I don't do ceilings'), seemed totally out of place in the light of what had gone before (and indeed behind). One can get so thrown.

My final word on the subject comes from Bangkok, where I was invited to speak recently at a Rotarian dinner. In his opening remarks my senior host told the assembled company, 'This is the oldest Rotarian club in Thailand and the most famous Rotarian club in Thailand. We have had here through the years since we were founded a lot of very distinguished guests [I meanwhile was preening and smiling modestly]. People of international renown. People of tremendous stature. And often I can say our guest today needs no introduction [more modest smiles from yours truly]. But nobody has ever heard of Derek Nimmo, so I will have to tell you all about him!'

Several years ago the guest of honour at a literary luncheon was forced to withdraw after suffering a mild nervous disorder a few weeks before the event. A substitute was found, but news arrived at the last moment that the original speaker felt sufficiently recovered to accept the invitation after all.

When the organizer arrived he found the guest of honour in deep conversation with an elderly lady of long acquaintance. 'Darling,' she greeted him as he went across to welcome them, 'I've just been explaining to this charming gentleman how our main speaker has gone off his rocker.'

Among Kenneth Williams's fund of stories was one told of a speaker at an all-male dinner, who, when asked by his wife what he was going to talk about, lied and said he was going to speak about flying.

'But you don't know the first thing about flying,' she reminded him.

'Never mind. I can mug something up,' was his

answer.

In fact he regaled his male colleagues with a succession of outrageous sexual anecdotes, which they all enjoyed hugely.

'Your husband spoke brilliantly, the other night,' enthused one of the audience when he next met the speaker's wife.

'Well, I must say I'm surprised,' she told him. 'He's only been up twice. The first time he was sick and the second time it blew his hat off.'

After-dinner speakers need to be wary of what they eat (not to say drink) at the meals which presage their speeches. From America comes the timely warning of a guest of honour at a very grand banquet who chewed a little too eagerly on one mouthful and cracked his dental plate. Calling the toastmaster as discreetly as the dilemma permitted, he whispered what had happened and asked, 'Can you think up some excuse? I can't possibly speak.'

His request met with an understanding smile and the toastmaster's hand proferring something under the table. It was a set of dentures.

Behind his napkin the speaker slipped these into his mouth. But they were too small.

Beneath the table he returned them to the toastmaster and was amazed to be offered a second set. These were too large.

Scarcely able to believe his luck two more sets were offered, the last of which fitted well enough for him to speak with confidence.

Thanking the toastmaster profusely afterwards, he added, 'What a piece of luck that you're a dentist.'

'I'm afraid I'm not,' the toastmaster told him. 'I'm an undertaker.'

It's hard to believe that a decade has passed since we were celebrating the engagement of the Prince of Wales to Lady Diana Spencer. For one loyal subject in Scotland, however, I suspect time's winged chariot couldn't hurry along quickly enough. This was the fellow who found himself with the good fortune of congratulating the Prince in person a few days after the official announcement, when he welcomed him to a lunch held by businessmen north of the border. Raising his glass he invited all present to drink to the health and happiness of 'Prince Charles and Lady Jane'!

The eighteenth-century politician John Wilkes was dining once with an earlier Prince of Wales, the one who later became George IV. During the course of the meal, to quote the eighteenth-century Lord Eldon, whose anecdote this is, 'Wilkes overheard the Prince talking of him pretty freely.'

This was at the time when the expression of 'sentiments' was coming into fashion in place of traditional toasts drunk to the health of the fair sex. So when Wilkes was called on for his sentiment, he gave, 'The King, and long may he live.'

This came as rather a surprise to the Prince Regent, who asked, 'Why, when did you become so loyal?'

'Ever since I had the honour of knowing your Royal Highness,' answered Wilkes.

A former American ambassador to the Court of St James's was invited to an important dinner in the City. He was in the process of examining the menu card when he was informed that his hosts expected him to speak afterwards.

'Sir,' he replied, 'to my whitebait you have now added my *bête noire*.'

Thirty years ago Dame Kathleen Lonsdale was invited to propose the toast to the official guest at an annual dinner of the British Association held in Cardiff. She took the opportunity to suggest that the ideal toast should be similar to a remark she had recently overheard on a London bus crossing Battersea Bridge. There a woman on the lower deck rose to her feet and shouted, 'I have had three husbands.'

Her statement was succinct, it raised immediate interest in further details and she sat down.

F E Smith, or Lord Birkenhead, to give him his ennoblement, was speaking at Cambridge on one occasion when a faint voice from the back of his audience interrupted him in full spate.

The great man stopped in his tracks. An awful silence descended.

'Stand up, sir,' ordered F E, and a cowering figure in a tattered gown rose at the end of the hall.

There was another terrible silence.

Then F E boomed down the hall, 'Sit down, sir. The insignificance of your appearance is sufficient answer to the impudence of your interruption', and as the heckler gratefully resumed his seat, the whole hall roared with delighted relief.

The Prince of Wales (later to become the Duke of Windsor) and Lord Birkenhead were guests of honour at the official opening of a new town hall in Brighton. One of the speakers droned tediously on to the point where the Prince whispered to F E, 'Can't we dry this fellow up?'

'Leave it to me,' was the answer.

The Prince saw his companion scribble a note which he then handed to the toastmaster, who placed it discreetly in front of the speaker. The effect was instantaneous and dramatic. The speech ended almost immediately and the speaker fairly dropped into his seat, his eyes apparently fixed on the table.

'What did you write?' whispered the Prince of Wales.

'Told him his fly buttons were open,' answered F E.

The search for oratorical elegance can occasionally lead to unfortunate turns of phrase. A British envoy, recently arrived at a new posting in the orient, was invited to propose a toast to the ladies at a banquet held in his honour. Seeking words that he hoped would be warmly received by guests from both east and west, he offered a toast to 'the two hemispheres of ladies'.

Then there was the case of the diplomat attending a trade delegation dinner in Leningrad, before the days of *glasnost*. He thought he'd try proposing the health of his hosts in their native tongue. An hour or so with a phrasebook and a bit of help from the official interpreter gave him a respectable little address that should have warmed Soviet hearts. Sadly, when he rose to his feet his mind went blank and the opening words, 'Ladies and gentlemen', flew from his mind. Calling on all his diplomatic savoir-faire, he cast his eyes winningly over the assembled company until they alighted on the two words he was seeking, printed in bold Cyrillic letters above two doors at the back of the room.

In spite of this chance discovery, the toast somehow failed to achieve its desired effect and the speaker confided his disappointment to a colleague on their way home.

'It's probably because you began by addressing them as male and female conveniences', he was told.

An ambassador from one of the countries that we used to look upon as being behind the Iron Curtain was speaking in London one evening and opened by reassuring his audience that he would be obeying Lord Reading's dictum that, 'An after-dinner speech should be shorter than anyone dared hope.'

'I am not wanting to make too long a speech tonight,' said the ambassador, 'because I know your English saying, "Early to bed and up with the cock."'

Dame Rebecca West was once seated next to Sir Winston Churchill at a dinner where the guest speaker, another politician, talked on at tedious length. At one point she leant across to Sir Winston and whispered, 'Now I can say with perfect truth that you and I have slept together.'

I remember driving Rebecca West, about a year before her death, to Michael Denison and Dulcie Gray's house just outside Amersham, and on the way down in the car she said to me, 'You know, I always remember Bernard Shaw's wife telling me how he came to write *St Joan*.' She went on to say that Mrs Shaw had suggested the idea several times as a good subject for a play, but Shaw had pooh-poohed it, as he pooh-poohed every suggestion she made. Knowing that he always spent a great deal of time every day in the loo, she gathered together every book she could find about St Joan and put them in there. Over a period of months Shaw worked his way through them and emerged one day to tell her that he'd got a wonderful idea for a play about Joan of Arc.

What bearing Shaw's vegetarianism had on the evolution of this masterpiece can only be conjectured.

When he was quite well advanced in years A E Matthews, known throughout the theatre as Matty, was invited to a large luncheon held in the grounds at Pinewood. Lunch was followed by a number of delightful speeches, all but one of which followed Rab Butler's celebrated dictum on toasts: that they should be like a woman's dress – long enough to cover everything but short enough to be interesting. The exception was the last speaker, the head of finance or something like that. To pursue the couturial metaphor, his speech was dressed in mourning from head to foot. Everyone became restless, but it was Matty who spoke for them all when he announced loudly, 'Good Lord, doesn't the fellow realize I haven't got long to live?'

The American playwright and humorist George Ade was always a popular after-dinner speaker and, following one of his speeches, an eminent lawyer picked on this when he rose to speak as the applause for George Ade died away.

Standing with hands buried in his trouser pockets, the lawyer asked, 'Doesn't it strike the company as a little unusual that a professional humorist should be funny?'

That earned him the laugh he had hoped for. But as it died away, Ade countered with a question of his own: 'Doesn't it strike the company as a little unusual that a lawyer should have his hands in his own pockets?'

A dinner was given by the University of London in 1911 to bid farewell to A E Housman, who was leaving the Chair of Latin there to take up a similar post at Cambridge as the Kennedy Professor of Latin. Commenting on his future home, Housman told his audience, 'The University which once saw Wordsworth drunk and once saw Porson sober will see a better scholar than Wordsworth, and a better poet than Porson, betwixt and between.'

I believe it was Denis Healey who once recounted a salutary speaking experience of one of his predecessors as chancellor of the exchequer. This particular chancellor found it difficult to compose his own after-dinner speeches and got into the habit of delegating the task to his private secretary – often at rather short notice. For some years this arrangement seemed to work quite well and the chancellor achieved a modest reputation as a witty and engaging speaker. Then one evening he met his nemesis.

Rising to address a civic gathering somewhere in the north, he began confidently: 'My Lord Mayor, Lady Mayoress, Ladies and Gentlemen. The problem which faces us today is one of the most daunting that our nation has ever encountered. Unless we can find a solution in the coming months, the future looks sombre and our fortunes stark. I foresee only two options open to us as we address these grave issues . . .'

Then he turned over the page and continued reading, 'From now on, you're on your own, you bastard.'

During his time as Minister for the Arts, Norman St John Stevas was invited to speak at the Museum of the Year award lunch. Towards the end of his speech he reportedly told his audience, 'But I mustn't go on singling out names . . . One mustn't be a name-dropper, as Her Majesty remarked to me yesterday.'

Demon Drink

I was slaking my thirst once in a bar in Barbados when my attention was momentarily distracted from the glass before me by these thought-provoking lines:

> The horse and mule live thirty years,
>   They never tasted wines or beers.
> Sheep and goats are dead at twenty.
> They drink no liquor, water plenty.
>   At fifteen dogs are mostly dead,
> They look not on the wine when red.
> At ten, cats have lost all nine lives,
> No beast on milk and water thrives.
> At five, most birds have passed away,
>   Far from alcohol they stay.
> Bugs spend but few days on this earth,
> They never saw the cocktail's worth.
> But ginful, sinful, rum-soaked men,
>   Live on three-score years and ten.

Now, I'd venture to suggest that few sonnets (which by convention contain the same number of lines) hold truths of greater universal application. Having sampled willingly all over the world of Keats's 'draught of vintage! that hath been/Cool'd a long age in the deep-delv'd earth', not to mention some younger and more spirited concoctions, I am inclined to concur with Sir Winston Churchill's remark, 'Always remember, I have taken more out of alcohol than alcohol has taken out of me.'

I enjoy drinking, frequently in the company of good food, and firmly cleave to the time-honoured maxim that one swallow doesn't make a summer. I must confess to having drawn the line at sampling a bat cocktail in Bangkok, for the simple reason that, exotic as the name may sound, it is all too accurate a description – for bat cocktail is exactly what it is. The bats are actually hanging upside down at the back of the restaurant, minding their own business until someone places an order for one of these macabre drinks. Rather like choosing one's trout or lobster before it is dispatched to the kitchen, you select your bat and then leave it to the waiters to spirit it away and return shortly with your drink containing a hefty shot of the poor mammal's blood. Drink too many, and you end up looking like Christopher Lee.

Travel, while broadening the mind, also greatly enriches the palate and my many visits to Australia have been accompanied by the happy discovery of the superb wines produced there. Some of my favourite red wines come from Australia. Indeed, once upon a time I was the proud possessor of a dozen bottles of the truly magnificent 1961 Grange Hermitage – though that is a sorry tale.

The bottles had been given to me as a present, a charming and generous gesture in itself. Together we travelled from Adelaide to Melbourne, from Melbourne to Hobart, from Hobart to Launceston, from Launceston to Canberra, from Canberra to Singapore and from Singapore to Dubai. Thus far my precious cargo winged its way from place to place totally unscathed. Only when we landed in dear old Blighty, a mere matter of a few miles from my welcoming cellar, did the unthinkable happen. Borne from aircraft hold to customs hall on the suitcase-devouring conveyor belt at Heathrow, their fate was sealed. By the time I reached the case, battered and spilling forth its matchless contents, only four bottles remained intact. Every sip from one of the survivors seemed like a toast to absent friends.

While wine will always remain my first love, there are those occasions when one's tastebuds feel the need of different stimuli and here a cocktail can be wonderfully rewarding.

I'm particularly partial to a really good Bloody Mary, which I enjoy on the strong side. I like to use Clamato (tomato juice with clam juice in it), to which I add Tabasco, Worcestershire sauce, oregano and salt and pepper. To this I add grated fresh horseradish (which makes it a pretty fiercesome brew by this time), before floating the vodka on the top like cream. I enjoy sipping my drink through the vodka, though others make use of a long carrot to stir theirs. Those are fun to chew when you've finished.

For all its faults, Christianity does at least permit its followers the occasional (or in the case of the truly devout, the daily) drop of vino. The same, of course, cannot be said for the followers of Islam, a fact which might have appeared to have been a major impediment to the late Aga Khan, who habitually enjoyed life and all its riches to the full. However, Allah in his mercy endowed the spiritual head of the Ismaili sect with a divine dispensation that turned wine into milk as it entered his mouth, thus allowing him to replenish his cellar at regular intervals without the slightest hint of disapproval from on high.

Now that *glasnost* seems set to open up the frontiers of the Soviet Union to western travellers, prospective visitors might care to be cautioned on the subject of their would-be hosts' capacity for drinking – and drinking deep. Getting on for a century ago, the then Duke of Edinburgh, brother to King Edward VII, offered this advice on how to enjoy Russian hospitality without succumbing to the inevitable retribution of the bottle. 'Whenever I am invited to dine on a Russian ship,' he confided to a friend, 'I always take the precaution of drinking half a liqueur glass of salad oil, just before I start. I can then drink brandy to their claret and drink them all under the table. The oil prevents any fumes rising to the brain, so that I remain perfectly sober. Of course, I take a strong purge directly I get back.'

❈

From all accounts Ben Jonson was not averse to a glass of wine now and then. Inviting a friend to supper in verse, he acknowledged:

> But that which doth take my Muse and me,
> Is a pure cup of rich Canary wine,
> Which is the Mermaid's now, but shall be mine.

His major problem seems to have been matching his means to his consumption. At one stage he was rather heavily in debt to a wine merchant – not that this appeared to sour their relationship, for the vintner happily invited Jonson to dine with him and displayed no frugality when passing the bottle.

Jonson must have been on uncommonly good form that evening, for the vintner suggested after several bottles that he would write off all the poet's debts if Jonson could immediately answer the questions: 'What God is best pleased with? What the devil is best pleased with? What the world is best pleased with? And what he was best pleased with?'

Rising to the occasion, and perhaps mindful of the first two lines above, Jonson immediately responded with a pair of charming couplets:

> God is best pleased when men forsake their sin;
> The devil's best pleased when they persist therein;
> The world's best pleased when thou dost sell good wine;
> And you're best pleased when I do pay for mine.

The English chronicler Raphael Holinshed was an enthusiastic advocate of whisky, and back in the reign of Good Queen Bess, when not all things Scots were looked on as favourably as they are today, he offered these reasons for sipping a dram now and then:

> Being moderately taken it sloweth age, it strengtheneth youth, it helpeth digestion, it cutteth flegme, it lighteneth the mind, it quickeneth the spirits, it cureth hydropsie, it pounceth the stone, it expelleth gravell, it puffeth away ventositie, it keepeth the weason from stifling, the stomach from wambling, the heart from swelling, the bellie from wirtching, the guts from numbling, the hands from shivering and the sinews from shrinking, the veins from crumbling, the bones from aking and the marrow from soaking.

The eighteenth-century Irish orator John Philpot Curran suggested that there were three reasons for not drinking too much: first the sin; second the shame; and third the sickness.

'Claret', said Dr Johnson, 'is the liquor for boys, port for men; but he who aspires to be a hero must drink brandy.'

In 1785 *The Times* carried this dire warning about certain London watering holes:

> Attention is to be paid to gin-shops, alias Wine Vaults; each of these is a Pandora's box, pregnant with evils and diseases. It is in these places the murderer and robber irradicate the feelings of human nature, by the use of spiritous liquors; it is here they stimulate the minds to acts of horror; it is here the tradesman's wife squanders the earnings of her husband; it is from these shops the abandoned prostitute issues into the streets, to seduce the innocence of youth from the path of virtue.
>
> A visitation should be repeatedly made to a coffee house not a hundred miles from Soho, where demireps hold nocturnal revels, and where every species of debauchery is practised.

When Pepsi Cola made its first appearance in the People's Republic of China the company's advertising team decided they couldn't improve on the slogan that had won impressive sales in the west.

So 'Come alive with Pepsi' became the touchstone for the marketing onslaught on the 'Middle Kingdom' and one in five of the Earth's population.

When east meets west, however, it doesn't always follow that there is a complete meeting of minds. At least there wasn't in this case. For in translation the memorable Pepsi slogan managed to acquire rather sinister overtones and came out something like, 'Pepsi brings your ancestors back from the grave.'

One of the ushers at a wedding was wandering among the guests, few of whom he knew and fewer still was able to remember, thanks to the considerable quantities of wine both sparkling and table that had passed between his lips. Catching a conversation on the merits of buying a holiday home in Wales, he heard himself loudly offering the opinion, 'There are only two worthwhile things that come out of Wales – rugby players and prostitutes.'

One of the other guests, a giant of a man with a broken nose and other signs of past physical encounters, turned on him menacingly and said, 'My wife was born and bred in Wales.'

The usher's wits were rapidly recalled from the revels and he heard himself asking, 'Oh really, and what position did she play?'

The occasional murmurings of dissent one hears about the varying approaches taken by magistrates in different parts of the country seem to have some substance when you consider two rather unlikely applications to sell alcohol. One was made to magistrates in Kent by the organizers of a celebration to mark the first anniversary of a local club. This was queried by the bench when the organization in question was revealed to be the Sheerness Temperance Club. On the other hand, magistrates 100 miles away in Oxfordshire felt able to grant a drinks extension to the Bell Hotel in Charlbury for a dinner dance organized by Alcoholics Anonymous.

A new barman in a pub near Aylesbury was asked whether he had any half Coronas. This threw him for a minute until enlightment dawned and he asked brightly, 'Orange or lemon, sir?'

There's a London pub that has a large and impressive vine growing in its courtyard. One year this produced a handsome harvest of grapes, which the landlord felt moved to make into wine. This was duly offered to customers once it had been bottled and met with a mixed response. One lady invited to sample the vintage, swallowed it with distaste and asked, 'Where did you say this came from?'

'Out there', said the landlord, pointing outside.

'Doesn't travel very well, does it?' said the lady.

In the summer of 1953 Mr Juan Martinez, a sixty-four-year-old Puerto Rican, boarded a plane at New York en route for his home city of San Juan. Speaking no language but Spanish, he brandished his boarding card and relied on others to show him where to go. What he didn't realize was that the card showed no flight number and by mistake he was helped on board a plane bound for the West German city of Frankfurt. Not long after take-off a stewardess asked in English whether he would care for a drink.

'Martinez,' he answered, thinking she had asked him his name, and found himself presented with the unexpected bonus of a cocktail.

This happened several more times on the flight north, so that when the plane landed at Gander in Newfoundland, Mr Martinez might as well have been in Puerto Rico for all he cared. In spite of the airline's hospitality, he was still aware of an unusually bracing feel to the air for a Caribbean July and shortly afterwards the 180° error in his flight was detected. Following a night's rest in a hotel (again at the airline's expense), he was put on board a flight back to New York, where he was transferred to a connecting flight to San Juan, eager to tell anxious relatives about the remarkable generosity the airline had shown him, though still mystified as to why his return flight had taken three times longer than the one that had taken him to New York in the first place.

Dorothy Parker once gave a party at which Tallulah Bankhead drank a trifle too much and consequently behaved rather indecorously. When the time came for her to be escorted home, Dorothy Parker called after the departing figure, 'Has Whistler's mother left yet?'

The next morning it is reported that Miss Bankhead peered blearily into a compact mirror and then said to Dorothy Parker, 'The less I behave like Whistler's mother the night before, the more I look like her the morning after.'

Brahms was invited to dinner by a man famous for his knowledge of wine and the cellar that he had created. In honour of the composer's visit the connoisseur brought out some of his very best vintages. As he offered his distinguished guest a glass from one venerable bottle, he announced, 'This is the Brahms of my cellar.'

The composer examined his namesake carefully,

inhaled its bouquet, sipped it and then put down his glass without a word.

'How do you like it?' inquired his host.

'Better bring out your Beethoven,' said Brahms.

Anthelme Brillat-Savarin, the author of the famous classic of gastronomy *Physiologie du goût*, was asked by a lady whether he preferred Burgundy or claret. He replied, 'That, madame, is a question that I take so much pleasure in investigating that I postpone from week to week the pronouncement of a verdict.'

John Timbs, writing in his anthology *A Century of Anecdote* more than a century ago, records this story told of the playwright Richard Brinsley Sheridan:

Sheridan was dining with Lord Thurlow, when his Lordship produced some fine Constantia, which had been sent to him from the Cape of Good Hope. The wine tickled the palate of Sheridan, who saw the bottle emptied with uncommon regret, and set his wits to work to get another. The old Chancellor was not to be so easily induced to produce his curious Cape in such profusion, and foiled all attempts to get another glass. Sheridan, being piqued, and seeing the inutility of persecuting the immovable pillar of the law, turned towards a gentleman seated further down, and said, 'Sir, pass me up that decanter; for I must return to Madeira, since I cannot double the Cape.'

In the summer of 1846 the *Essex Standard* reported these unexpected consequences from a refreshing glass of beer:

The wife of Mr Strutt, the sexton of St Peter's Parish, Colchester, had a narrow escape from death on Sunday week, by accidentally swallowing a wasp with some beer which she was drinking. The insect in passing down her throat stung it severely, without, however, leaving its sting in the wound; fortunately the windpipe escaped uninjured, or death must have ensued, but it renewed its attack upon her stomach, occasioning great pain; medical aid was soon procured, and a powerful emetic, administered by Mr Charles Murray, providentially affected speedy dislodgement of the wasp, though it was alive and vigorous when ejected from the stomach.

✳

In the course of a royal visit to the Bahamas the Queen noticed her host take a silver pencil from his pocket to swizzle the bubbles out of a drink. Amused at this, she inquired, 'That's all right in our company, but what happens in high society?'

During their 1939 tour of the United States Her Majesty's parents were offered cocktails mixed by their host, Franklin D Roosevelt. The president's mother joined the party and watched her son mixing the drinks with disapproval. 'My mother thinks I should be offering you a cup of tea,' he explained. 'She doesn't approve of cocktails.'

'Neither does my mother,' said King George VI, accepting the drink gratefully.

At the time that Napoleon Bonaparte held sway in France, Frederick Augustus I ruled the kingdom of Saxony. Like many monarchs of his day he was partial to a drop of wine and so, it seemed, was the royal barber. One day both were engaged in the royal ablutions when the barber accidentally nicked the king's chin and shed several drops of the blood blue.

'That comes from all that damned wine,' yelled Frederick Augustus.

'Unfortunately true, Your Majesty,' said the barber. 'Alcohol does tend to dry the skin.'

The Irish poet Oliver St John Gogarty went into a pub one day, saw a fellow drinker with a patch over one eye and hailed him with the cheerful words, 'Drink to me with thine only eye.'

As a most enjoyable dinner party neared its end, the early-nineteenth-century journalist Theodore Hook noticed that one of his fellow guests, a bookseller by trade, had evidently consumed more than his share of wine. 'You appear to have emptied your wine cellar into your bookseller,' whispered Hook to his host.

The eighteenth-century Irish politician Sir Hercules Langrishe shared an enthusiasm for port frequently associated with diners of his day. However, even he aroused admiration in polishing off three bottles at a sitting. Asked if he had had any help in this feat, he replied, 'None – save that of a bottle of Madeira.'

✳

Richard Porson is probably the most famous eighteenth-century English scholar, celebrated both for his erudition and for his extraordinary capacity for drink. Among the stories of his devotion to the bottle is that centred on a visit he paid to the portrait painter John Hoppner. Porson arrived unannounced and, pleased though his friend was to see him, the house was ill-prepared to entertain a guest of Porson's reputation. For one thing Hoppner's wife was away and had taken the keys of the wine cupboard with her. This was a serious matter and, as the evening wore on, Porson's desire for a drink eventually drove him to suggest that his absent hostess must surely have hidden a bottle somewhere in her bedroom for her own private tippling.

Hoppner was a bit put out at this suggestion and was even more affronted when Porson returned triumphantly brandishing a bottle from the lady's boudoir, filled, he declared, with the finest gin he had ever tasted.

When Mrs Hoppner came home her husband told her crossly that Porson had found and drunk her secret hoard. 'Drunk it?' she answered in amazement. 'Good heavens – that was spirit of wine for the lamp.'

Porson might have sympathized with an Aberdeen man who was given four months in prison for stealing a gallon of his favourite tipple from a trawler moored in the city's harbour. What made this offence more than a little unusual was that the liquor to which he was so partial turned out to be the fluid used in ships' compasses.

A fellow Aberdonian was brought before another court in the city charged with causing a disturbance in a pub. Asked why he had found it necessary to bury a hatchet in the bar, he replied, 'I was having difficulty in catching the barmaid's attention.'

The cartoonist and short-story writer James Thurber was talking to a woman at a cocktail party who enthused about his work and went as far as to tell him that she found it even funnier in French than in English. 'Yes, I always seem to lose something in the original,' said Thurber.

Leaving a party where he had partaken enthusiastically of his host's food and wine, James Whistler said his farewells, which were followed a moment later by a loud crash as he fell down the stairs. When his host asked anxiously whether he was all right, Whistler asked the name of his architect. The man said that it was Norman Shaw, the prime mover in the trend away from Victorian styles and back to those of the Georgian era.

'I might have guessed it,' grumbled Whistler. 'The damned teetotaller.'

Police in the town of Corpus Christi, Texas, answered an emergency call and arrived at a house to find a furious woman demanding that they arrest her husband, who was slumped in a drunken stupor in his sitting-room. The officers told her that no law prevented a man from being drunk in his own home, in response to which she dragged the poor man out on to the pavement so that he could be arrested there.

For two years a draymen's strike in Birmingham prevented sales of beer in the Fox and Goose public house. Deliveries were reinstated only on Hallowe'en in 1977 and the landlord organized appropriate celebrations to mark the restoration of supplies. Then, barely a couple of minutes before opening-time on the appointed day, there was a power cut, which knocked out the electrically powered pumps.

Anyone concerned at the decline of small breweries producing 'real ale' in our present age might derive a modicum of comfort from an advertisement that appeared in *The Times* as long ago as 1822, which suggests that similar anxieties about the quality of ale were afoot even then:

To the admirers of the Genuine Home-Brewed, in the highest state of perfection: the general approbation so warmly bestowed upon the Home Brewed Ale, Stout and Porter, of the Bell Inn Brewery, Warwick Lane, having excited in many a desire to become acquainted with this brew and superior process of brewing from malt and hops only, W Bush begs to inform the County Brewers and Private Families, that he is willing to give instructions, on moderate terms, to such as will attend his brewings, where every information necessary to ensure a complete and practical knowledge of the process may be obtained.

The following reduction in prices has just taken place: Porter 4d, Stout 5d, Ale 6d per pot, and the same article sent in casks or bottles, according to order. Choice Wines and Spirits. Families supplied with Hops and Malt, ground or unground, in any quantity.

NB As the above are offered at a very small profit, no credit can be allowed.

Back in 1954 Rupert Denny, a former wine correspondent for the *Daily Telegraph*, took himself off to
Ireland for a fishing holiday and booked into a
small country hotel in County Galway.

Resigning himself to suffer the hotel's rather
meagre facilities in return for some excellent sport,
he went down to dinner on his first evening and
wasn't surprised to be presented with a pot of tea.

'I don't suppose you've got any wine?' he
ventured to ask, with no great sense of anticipation.

At first the waiter looked at him blankly and then
muttered that he thought there might be a few
bottles left in the cellar.

When he reappeared a considerable time later,
he was carrying an ancient handwritten wine list
that hadn't seen the light of day for many a year. Its
appearance was anything but auspicious and
Rupert Denny very nearly ignored it completely in
preference for the tea. Then a familiar name caught
his eye...then another...and another. The list,
old and decrepit as it was, listed some of the finest
pre-war vintages (and this was the part he could
scarcely believe) at their original pre-war prices.

Ordering a Hospice de Beaune 1935 at 14s 6d he
waited in an agony of anticipation and disbelief
while the waiter shuffled away again and finally
returned carrying a bottle as dusty as the wine list.
Nevertheless, when the grime was cleared from the
label the wine was revealed as the promised
vintage.

'Is it the right one, sir?' the waiter asked.

'Yes,' came the tremulous reply.

'In that case I'll just give it a good shake,' said the

waiter, obligingly upending the bottle. 'Sure all the goodness has gone to the bottom.'

During the last war Sir Winston Churchill was challenged by a member of his club about drinking a bottle of vintage hock.

'How can you possibly drink a German wine at a time like this?' Churchill was asked with a mixture of amazement and reproof.

'I'm not drinking it,' the prime minister replied gruffly. 'I'm interning it.'

Throughout the latter half of the eighteenth century Parson Woodforde kept a diary of life in his parish in East Anglia. Much of it is filled with details of what he ate and once in a while he gives his reader an insight into the way he spent his time replenishing his larder and cellar. After lunch on 20 October 1794, for example, he was busy brewing. This is what he got up to:

Busy most part of the Afternoon in making some Mead Wine, to fourteen Pound of Honey I put four Gallons of Water, boiled it more than an hour with Ginger and two handfulls of dried

Elder-Flowers in it, and skimmed it well. Then put it into a small Tub to cool, and when almost cold I put in a large gravey-Spoon full of fresh Yeast, keeping it in a warm place, the Kitchen during night.

He ends the entry for that day laconically: 'Dinner to day, Breast of Veal rosted [sic] &c.'

In 1825 Samuel and Sarah Adams published a handy little tome entitled *The Complete Servant*, which they filled with dozens of valuable tips for domestic staff, a good many of which referred to the preparation and care of drinks. Here are just three of the gems of advice they had to offer:

To Make Wine Settle Well

Take a pint of wheat and boil it in a quart of water, till it burst and become soft; then squeeze it through a linen cloth, and put a pint of liquor into the hogshead of unsettled white wine; stir it well about and it will become fine.

To Detect Adulterated Wine

Heat equal parts of oyster-shells and sulphur together, and keep them in a white heat for fifteen minutes, and when cold, mix them with an equal quantity of cream of tartar; put this mixture into a strong bottle with common water to boil for one hour, and then decant into ounce phials, and add 20 drops of muriatic acid to each; this liquor precipitates the least quantity of lead, copper, &c. from wines in a very sensible black precipitate.

To Render Red Wine White

If a few quarts of well-skimmed milk be put to a hogshead of red wine, it will soon precipitate the greater part of the colour, and leave the whole nearly white; and this is of known use in the turning of red wines, when pricked, into white; in which a small degree of acidity is not so much perceived.

Milk is, from this quality of discharging colour from wines, of use also to the wine-coopers, for the whitening of wines that have acquired a brown colour from the cask, or from having been hastily boiled before fermenting; for the addition of a little skimmed milk, in these cases, precipitates the brown colour, and leaves wines of almost limpid, or of what they call a water whiteness, which is much coveted abroad in wines as well as brandies.

Thirty years ago an investigation was carried out to discover whether or not the noise generated at cocktail parties might constitute a health hazard to diplomats. The conclusion reached by the researchers was that at maximum volume the hubbub was not quite loud enough to cause permanent deafness.

As befitted the occasion, I discovered what must surely be the ultimate solution to hangovers at the Melbourne Cup. It was the fifth of these gloriously inebriated occasions that I had attended and after four I approached the next with a blend of foreboding and devil-may-care recklessness. The champagne starts flowing at nine in the morning, so a good part of the day passes in a delicious haze and the following day – well, that was another matter, for the first four visits at least.

Then I met Robert Sangster and he introduced me to some splendid Swiss tablets called Beroccas, which were sold under licence through an Australian company. The label said they were 'for use in deficiencies caused by infections, pregnancy, alcoholism or liver damage' - which makes them a panacea for all life's problems rolled into one. At the Melbourne Cup only one of these weighed on my mind, but by the following morning I felt as fresh as a daisy and my Melbourne Cup hath runneth over with joy ever since.

❋

When I first stayed at the Intercontinental Hotel in Muscat, quite a few years ago now, I couldn't help noticing that the bar seemed to be peopled by mysterious, craggy, deeply tanned men who were sitting on stools drinking what appeared to be rather large milk shakes. A discreet inquiry revealed that they were members of the SAS who were stationed down near the Yemeni border and who would come to Muscat for R & R. I also discovered that their curious tipple was known in those parts as a *Big Boy's Milk Shake*. It consisted of 4 cl of tequila and 2 cl of Kahlua, in a glass filled with ice-cold milk.

A man charged with being drunk in charge of a bicycle attempted to defend himself on the grounds that a bicycle could not be classified as a 'carriage'. If this was the case, it followed that he could not be found guilty of being 'drunk while in charge on any highway . . . of any carriage'.

While the reasoning of the latter argument might have been true, his initial premise did not impress the court – partly, one suspects, for the rather heavy reliance he placed on one verse of a popular song:

> It won't be a stylish marriage,
> I can't afford a carriage,
> But you'll look sweet upon the seat
> Of a bicycle made for two.

The landlady of a hotel in Ramsay, on the Isle of Man, fell foul of the law when she couldn't resist the urge to join customers in a singsong in the bar one evening. In her enthusiasm, she overlooked the trifling detail that her licence did not extend to singing. As the stipendiary magistrate who heard her case told her, by breaking into song she had 'abandoned the neutral attitude' that would otherwise have kept her within the law. Found guilty, she was fined 10s.

Mr Justice Swift was an enthusiastic servant of the bar in every sense and invariably looked indulgently on those with a similar affection for the bottle. On one occasion he presided over the case of a man arrested in the early hours of New Year's Day and charged with drunken driving. Under crossexamination the defendant admitted to having had a Scotch and soda at a New Year's Eve party and one for the road shortly after midnight.

'Now, members of the jury,' Swift began his summing-up, 'what are the facts? Why, this man had one drink in 1933 and didn't have another until 1934.'

It didn't take the jury long to return a verdict of 'Not guilty.'

Just Desserts?

I hope I can say without any hint of smugness that as a general rule food and drink have caused me very few problems down the years. Show me a menu in almost any language and I'll happily tuck into anything on it (well, almost anything). The same goes for the local brew, be that what it may, and with one or two notable exceptions most that I have sampled have left me relatively unscathed the following morning.

That said, Dame Fâte can keep some nasty tricks up her sleeve and I recall one particularly ghastly day twenty years ago when an apparently innocent bottle of cider and an otherwise unassuming meat pie contributed to a chapter of calamities of almost unimaginable proportions.

Let me explain.

It was ten in the morning in the Nimmo household and we were just about to leave to pick up our son Timothy from school so we could proceed *en famille* to open a fête in aid of some spectacularly worthy charity in one of the London suburbs.

I was about to close the front door when the telephone rang urgently behind me. It was Tim's housemaster, ringing to report that my first-born had knocked himself out at the termination of a fairly huge fall from the gymnasium's parallel bars. The upshot was that although he had recovered consciousness, he was now languishing in the sanatorium, confined to bed for twenty-four hours and nursing what was proclaimed to be a particularly effective black eye.

Obviously Tim wasn't leaving us in any doubt about his joining the outing. He was literally out!

We – that is, Yours Truly, wife Pat, daughter Amanda and Nimmo Minor, i.e. my baby son Piers – tried to set off for the second time, but as we did so Pat, in an awful moment, closed the door on Piers's hand.

There was a deal of blood, rather more shouting, and we hared off to the Outpatients department of the nearest hospital.

Considering he was only two, Piers was frightfully brave and after they had given him a local anaesthetic, they sewed up his hand with eight gory stitches. That nifty bit of surgical sewing would have done credit to the Royal School of Needlework!

We came back to the flat again – first, to check our growing family casualty list and, second, for Pat, who was fearfully upset, as you can imagine, to have a quick glass of something to restore her shattered nerves.

As soon as we were back through the doorway, Pat picked up the bottle of cider to which I made earlier reference. This promptly exploded, shooting glass in several directions and in the process cutting a two-inch-long gash on the top of her foot.

Once more Nimmo blood flowed freely and

206

some ten minutes after leaving Outpatients, we returned to be met by the same nurses, not only with disbelief but also with what sounded like several unseemly giggles.

Much to Piers's delight, he was able to sit and watch the doctor administer six more examples of his petit point.

The party going to the fête was now reduced to two, namely Amanda and myself. Furthermore, as I was due to open the proceedings in twenty-three minutes precisely, there was not time for anybody to indulge in the much-heralded lunch before the event.

We therefore grabbed two conveniently adjacent meat pies and sped off at a rate of knots, which isn't entirely to be recommended within a built-up area.

Just as we arrived at the fête, with some thirty seconds to spare, I took a final bite at the above-mentioned pie and to my absolute horror a tooth of which I had been particularly fond over the years broke in two . . .

But we Nimmos are a resilient lot and up I bounded on to the platform, regaled the gathered assembly with a little lighthearted repartee, declared the fête well and truly opened and told the audience how very sorry I was that I had had to leave my bleeding family at home.

As one who spent six years in *Charlie Girl* drinking a particularly nasty sort of ginger pop out of champagne bottles while trying to convey to the audience that I was cheerfully imbibing a merry glass of Dom Perignon's blessed creation, I can reliably confirm that stage food and drink aren't all that they seem.

However, it would be churlish of me not to acknowledge the great good fortune that that particular show brought me in so many ways. One of the most exciting days of my life was centred round it. While I was in Adelaide in January 1980 I found myself watching the exciting fifth test match with Neil Harvey seated on my left and Don Bradman on my right-hand side. As a schoolboy at an Old Trafford test I had tried to get Bradman's autograph on all five days, but it wasn't until all those years later that I finally got it in Adelaide. As we were talking, Bradman said, 'Look, Derek, I want to ask you something about that play you're in. You know when you drink some champagne, is it real or what?'

I told him about the ginger pop, but my head was spinning at the thought that 'Jehovah' had actually been to see me in a play. It was terribly exciting; the added joy was that England won the test by 205 runs.

Perhaps the organizers of an ingenious entertainment in South Australia a few years earlier might have benefited from sticking to more orthodox stage fare than that which they sought to provide. Backed by the state Arts Council, they conceived what you might call a 'dinner-drama' entitled *The Bard's Banquet*. It was a good idea and merited a better fate than the one dealt it.

The plot revolved around a jolly evening in the Elizabethan Mermaid Tavern, apparently a local watering-hole for the likes of Messrs Jonson, Marlowe and, of course, Shakespeare. Here the merry crew gathered for an evening's wining and dining, punctuated with songs of the day and merry tales about their respective lives. So far, so good. The subtlety of this show (and, one must admit, its undoing) was that while the cast were tucking into a five-course supper, the organizers planned to serve the audience with exactly the same fare. There was 300 in the house that night – and that's where the trouble started.

It wasn't until half-past ten, the time when most theatregoers would reckon to have left their seats and be into their first apéritif, that the audience's food arrived, 'by which time,' admitted one of the theatre staff, 'most of the audience were hungry and drunk. As the actors consumed their first course [potted shrimps],' he continued, 'several people of both sexes began to shout out that the food should be divided between the cast and the audience. And when Mr Bee [who was playing the part of Shakespeare] appealed for order, he was pelted with beer cans. By the time the roast ox was carried on, the audience had lost control. A man jumped on to the stage and began to throw portions of the ox into the auditorium. Then some of the crowd occupied the stage, threw the actors into the stalls, and fought hand-to-hand battles with those who had not managed to get so much as a piece of bread. One couple, shouting, "We don't care! We don't care!", began to make love in the middle of the fight; and, as the police had to drive fifty miles to reach the scene, nobody stopped them.'

A spokesman for the South Australia Arts Council who witnessed the 'performance' commented, 'It was a nightmare happening before my eyes. These people do not know what art is.'

One of the most dramatic episodes in the history of French cuisine came about in 1671 when Vatel, cook to the Prince de Condé, took his own life. According to contemporary reports, Vatel had been deeply upset one evening when his roast meat had run short during a dinner held in honour of the king. The following morning he was up early to ensure that such a disaster wasn't repeated, but on checking his provisions, he discovered to his horror that only two of the twelve carts of fish he had ordered had arrived. Overcome with despair he drew his sword and ran on it. His blood must still have been warm when the ten missing carts rumbled into the courtyard.

A shorthand typist working for a Darlington firm had the unnerving experience of turning everything she touched pink after eating a curry in one of the town's restaurants. Her clothes started to turn pink. Letters she typed took on a rose-coloured hue. So did her desk and office chair.

It took four days of laboratory tests to diagnose that one of the spices in the curry had produced a type of pink dye which found its way through the pores in her skin.

For ten years of his life Arnold Bennett lived in France. He married a Frenchwoman and, understandably, thought he knew the country pretty well. So when there was a public health scare in Paris while he was staying there in 1931, he sought to put friends at ease by assuring them that the tap water was safe to drink. To prove the point he knocked back a glassful, caught typhoid and died.

During one particularly bleak Parisian winter Ernest Hemingway eked out a hand-to-mouth existence trying and failing to sell his stories. He managed to keep his family fed only by poaching pigeons in the Luxembourg Gardens. He did this in the company of his infant son, while the policeman on duty was warming himself in a café. After luring the pigeons within reach with a handful of grain, Hemingway would deftly wring their necks and then hide them under the baby's pram blanket before wheeling them home to the pot.

A burglar who broke into a house on the outskirts of Paris was found fast asleep in one of the bedrooms the following morning. It appears that he had the misfortune to break into the kitchen, where a quick peep inside the fridge revealed a selection of excellent cheese and three bottles of champagne. With a conveniently adjacent baguette, these made a very agreeable preplundering picnic – by the end of which, however, the rest was silence.

I don't know whether it is still the case but at one time it was against the law in Ocean Beach, New York, to eat in a public place or to carry open containers of food. In a major crackdown against these particular felonies, police picked up one man for nibbling a chocolate biscuit, nabbed another for chewing a crumb cake and caught a third red-handed with a glass of water. The three defendants argued, not unreasonably, that there were dozens of people walking about eating ice creams with impunity. That, they were told, was a long-standing privilege enshrined in a by-law.

When an officer of the California highway patrol pulled over a motorist who had driven straight through a red light and asked the driver what he was up to, the man explained, 'If I make any sudden moves my wife spills her breakfast and that makes her mad.'

This unlikely state of affairs was confirmed by the presence of a lady sitting in the back seat, tucking into a plateful of bacon and eggs.

Failure to pay for his breakfast in a Birmingham café landed an eighty-six-year-old pensioner behind bars for the night – an experience that didn't altogether distress him. Told he could go the following morning, the old fellow refused point-blank to leave his cell. 'Anyone who has to struggle along on a pension would be mad to leave Winston Green,' he said. 'It's a real treat. Three square meals a day, central heating and plenty of new faces.'

The upshot was that he managed to prolong his stay for three months, shunning all efforts to get him out and only leaving when the prosecution applied for bail on his behalf.

'I was hoping to stay in for Christmas,' he said with disappointment. 'They say it's very, very good. Unfortunately, I'll just have to find a room elsewhere.'

The cost of his breakfast had been under 50p; his spell behind bars had set the taxpayer back not far short of £400.

A firm of food processors which was taken to court after a caterpillar had been found in a tin of its peas submitted the defence that this was 'an unavoidable consequence of the process of the collection or preparation of food'. The court thought the consequence was entirely avoidable and found against the plaintiff.

Alongside the names of the world's greatest cooks stands that of Mary Mallon, as well remembered for the particular qualities she brought to her kitchen as Carème, Escoffier and the rest brought to theirs. Mary came to public notice in the early years of this century. In the summer of 1906 she was engaged to cook in a wealthy New York household and one steaming-hot day prepared a dinner of icy-cold Nantucket cucumber soup, lobster thermidor served with rice and cold champagne on a dish of local oysters baked in their shells. The meal was a triumph and none of the guests suspected it when ten days later several of them were taken to hospital feeling distinctly unwell. There they were diagnosed as suffering from typhoid. Typhoid Mary Mallon had struck again.

By the time Dr George Soper of the New York City Department of Health had figured out the connection between the cook and the ailing guests, Mary Mallon had moved on and in fact had disappeared off the face of the earth. In her absence Dr Soper started to piece together an alarming trail that zigzagged across the north-east of the USA. Mary appeared to change jobs fairly regularly and her departure from each post was soon followed by outbreaks of typhoid.

In the end Dr Soper tracked down his quarry, confronted her with his evidence and pleaded with her, as the first known typhoid carrier in the country, to submit herself to treatment. She responded with a rolling-pin with which she chased Dr Soper from the kitchen – and that was more or less the way that she and the public health authorities coexisted for the next thirty years.

After spending an enforced year in hospital, where it was confirmed beyond doubt that she was riddled with typhoid and, while feeling as fit as a fiddle herself, was a living menace to the rest of the human race, she won her freedom, changed her name to lose the press sobriquet 'Typhoid Mary' and disappeared once more. The authorities had wrung from her the promise to give up cooking or handling any foods, but after five years it became evident that Mary Mallon had not stuck to this when another serious outbreak of typhoid was reported in the Sloane Hospital for Women. Twenty-five nurses and attendants were taken ill and two of the patients died. As usual, Mary Mallon had moved on by this time but, with the police alerted nationwide, she was soon cornered, again working in a kitchen.

This time there was no escape and for the rest of her life she was confined in a hospital on North Brother Island, where she stubbornly refused any treatment until her death at the age of seventy, when a severe stroke carried her off.

When is a fish not a fish? The answer, according to one legal case in Scotland, would seem to be when it's a prawn. This interesting philosophical question arose when an employee in a fish factory in Eyemouth was charged with ill-treating the prawns she converted into scampi. The nub of the case against her rested on the undeniable fact that she had placed the prawns on a hotplate and at first she was content to plead guilty. However, her counsel was less sanguine and advised her to change her plea.

Referring to the 1912 Protection of Animals (Scotland) Act, he argued that 'animals' were classified as any domestic or captive animal;

prawns didn't get a mention.

Furthermore, he reminded the court that the same act referred elsewhere to birds, fish and reptiles in captivity. For a prawn to be classified as a fish as defined in that act, he argued that it had to be one in 'captivity' – in other words, one living in an aquarium or similar aquatic enclosure. In support of his case he went on to tell the court that in a standard work of natural history nowhere was a prawn classified as a fish.

His reasoning, though possibly baffling to his client, at least found a sympathetic ear in the presiding sheriff, who told the court that if the evidence showed that a prawn was not a fish, the prosecution would have some difficulty in furthering its case!

The Irish politician James Molyneaux suffered exquisite embarrassment when he called in to visit one of his Antrim constituents and was offered a cup of tea in the parlour. On the way up to the farmhouse he had been greeted by a large, lively dog, which ran in front and preceded him into the parlour. As the MP and the farmer's wife nibbled biscuits and sipped their tea, the dog careered around the room, leaping on to the soft cushions with its muddy paws and knocking over lamps and side tables.

Slightly surprised that the farmer's wife didn't put a stop to the mayhem, the politician plodded gamely on, aware of a growing chill in the atmosphere. It was soon clear that the time had come for him to go and, with rather hurried thanks for the tea, he saw himself out.

Walking away from the house, he was horrified to hear a voice calling after him, 'Aren't you going to take your dog with you?'

The relationship between one's diet and the law may not appear to be that close at first sight but one case presented in court by the eminent American lawyer Samuel Leibowitz had farreaching implications that amounted to a matter of life and death.

This was a murder case in which Leibowitz's client claimed that he had been working in a fish market at the time the crime was committed. The prosecution sought to disprove his alibi by bringing a selection of fish into court and asking the defendant to identify them. He didn't know the name of a single one and when Leibowitz rose to make his final submission to the jury, things looked decidedly black for the man in the dock.

He opened his address by speaking to individual members of the jury, 'I want you, Mr Rabinowitz, and you, Mr Epstein, and you, Mr Goldfogel, and you, Mr Ginsberg, to explain to your fellow jurymen the fraud which has been perpetrated on my client. You see through it; they do not. Was there in all that array of fish a single pike, or pickerel, or any other fish that can be made into gefilte fish? There was not. My client told you that he worked in a store in 114th Street and Lexington Avenue. The prosecutor knows that this is a Jewish neighbourhood, and he did not show a single fish that makes gefilte fish. What a travesty of justice! My client is an Italian who works in a Jewish fish market, and they try him on Christian fish.'

After that the jury had little trouble in reaching a verdict and Leibowitz's client was acquitted unanimously.

A day or two after magistrates in Shropshire fined a local supplier of 'fresh produce' £300 for poaching, notices began appearing in the neighbourhood around Market Drayton to the effect that, due to unforeseen circumstances, he had been obliged to increase the price of pheasant, partridge, rabbit, hare and venison.

Some curious laws relating to food have been encoded around the world. At one time it was illegal to eat snakes on a Sunday in Iraq. In 1910 the good people of Waterloo, Nebraska, passed a by-law prohibiting barbers from eating onions between the hours of seven in the morning and seven in the evening. And three years later the state legislature in North Dakota ruled that, 'Every person who offers to sell any beef and fails to exhibit to the purchaser on demand the hide of the animal to be sold, and does not keep such hide for ten days after the sale, at his place of residence, or refuses to allow the same to be inspected by any person, is punishable.'

School food has always suffered from a rather dubious (and I daresay largely apocryphal) reputation. However, there was an occasion in a Welsh school when the zeal of public health inspectors may have been just a little misplaced.

At the centre of the controversy was a consignment of corned beef. Members of staff thought it smelt slightly questionable. The canteen major-domo had a sniff and passed it. The enviromental health officer, called in to give his opinion, sniffed it and passed it as well. Just to be on the safe side, the district medical officer was invited to offer his olfactory verdict. He also said that the corned beef smelt all right – only he went on to order that it be destroyed. Apparently too many people had sniffed it.

William Beckford, author of the Gothic novel *Vathek* and an eccentric builder able to indulge a passion for the grandiose with a fortune to match, was not a man who enjoyed company. One of the first things he did when returning to the family seat at Fonthill in Wiltshire after several years abroad was to construct a wall 12 feet high and 7 miles long right around his estate to keep out prying eyes. Then he got to work building a folly, 'a convent, partly in ruins and partly perfect'. However, his mercurial spirit soon inspired him to bolder plans and the folly rapidly turned into a complete abbey, surmounted by a 300-foot-high octagonal tower.

Apart from the hoard of workmen (never fewer than 100 at a time) no one saw the abbey, though many were eager to. Then one young man scaled the walls for a bet and was shown round the gardens and house by a man whom he assumed to be the gardener. However, his obliging guide turned out to be Beckford himself, who, after giving his unexpected visitor a genial tour of his home, invited him to dinner – a gesture which was quite at odds with the reputation by which he was known outside his walls. The meal was superb, Beckford proved himself to be a courteous and generous host, and his young guest felt at ease with the world when his host excused himself at the end of the meal and disappeared for some considerable time. In fact, he didn't appear again. In the end it was a servant who escorted the young man to the front door and said, 'Mr Beckford ordered me to present his compliments to you, sir, and I am to say that as you found your way into Fonthill Abbey without assistance, you may find your way out as best you can; and he hopes you will take care to avoid the bloodhounds that are let loose in the garden every night.'

With that the door was slammed shut behind him and Beckford's guest made a terrified dash to the nearest tree, in whose branches he spent a wretched time until daylight, when he made good his escape.

DEREK NIMMO

UP MOUNT EVEREST WITHOUT A PADDLE

A little travelling music, maestro, please ... Derek Nimmo offers an in-flight feast of traveller's tales with the maximum duty-free allowance of laughter.

Travelwise enough to avoid such hazards as playing in *There's a Girl in My Soup* in Papua New Guinea, the long-distance Nimmo is no stranger to the traumas of travel. Indeed, his first flight on a Jumbo was sadly marred when he was told: 'I'm sorry sir, you can only see a dirty movie if you're a smoker.'

His gloriously funny global guide is spiced with such gems overheard as the American lady's complaint on ascending the Parthenon – 'You'd think with all these tourists about, they would build an elevator . . .'

HODDER AND STOUGHTON PAPERBACKS

DEREK NIMMO

AS THE ACTRESS SAID TO THE BISHOP

Derek Nimmo has an actor's eye and ear for the odd incident and the bizarre story. He has played many roles and done many things – some of them strange in the extreme.

Showbusiness is an overflowing world of unlikely characters, farcical scenes and comic happenings. Here are stories of the big names, the bit players and the whole improbable off-stage cast: the eccentric landladies, over-sensitive writers, manic agents, erratic promptors, uncontrollable props and mad stage managers.

Together they add up to an hilarious collection of anecdotes from stage and screen, all told in the inimitable Nimmo style.

HODDER AND STOUGHTON PAPERBACKS